Jamie,
Keep Stepping forward in
He will use the
in our lives & turn
Triumphs! Out of you
His glory that will
you, guide you, anoint you
I love you "Daisy"
Jennifer
"Petrina"

MEMORIES

&

MILESTONES

Stepping Forward by Looking Back

Jennifer J. Pasquale

Jennifer J. Pasquale, Publisher

Copyright © 1997

by Jennifer J. Pasquale, Publisher

All rights reserved. No part of this publication may be reproduced in any form by any means, electronic, mechanical, photocopy, recording or otherwise, without the prior permission of the publisher.

Jennifer J. Pasquale

Commerce Township, Michigan 48382

Cover Design: Epoch Designs, Luis Lopez

ISBN 0-9658095-4-4

DEDICATION

This book is dedicated to my Lord, my Saviour, my Friend, Jesus Christ, for all the memories He's seen me through and for being the Cornerstone of all my milestones. May the words of this book bring others closer to their relationship with HIM!

ACKNOWLEDGMENTS

* I wish to thank all of my family and friends who have supported me in this endeavor and encouraged me through each of the milestones of my life. Without their encouragement, I would not have had a story to tell.

* I want to personally thank Steve Hill and his staff for guiding me through the publishing process and giving me assistance whenever I needed it. Thank you!

* Luis Lopez who worked continuously with me on the cover design until we got it just right. Thanks, Luis, for putting my thoughts onto paper.

* Special thanks to Jackie Elmore and Lisa Nagel for their secretarial assistance.

* My deepest gratitude goes to my brother-in-law, Todd Pasquale for his financial support of this project which made this dream a reality. I love you!

* Thank you Daddy, for encouraging me to write and take steps of faith!

* Thank you to my three beautiful daughters, for their patience and support during all the long hours of typing, papers everywhere, laughing, crying, and remembering. They fill my life with joy!

* And my wonderful husband, Rick. I could never have accomplished this project without his support, encouragement, guidance, and love. You have always nurtured my ministry and I love you more than words can say!

CONTENTS

Acknowledgments 9
Foreword 13
Prologue 15
Chapter 1   *Survival 101* 17
Chapter 2   *The Foundational Years* 19
Chapter 3   *What is a Memory?* 23
Chapter 4   *Remembering Momma* 27
Chapter 5   *The Car Wreck* 31
Chapter 6   *What is a Milestone?* 39
Chapter 7   *Changes* 41
Chapter 8   *Daddy* 49
Chapter 9   *Meeting "Mr. Right"* 55
Chapter 10   *Before "I Do"* 61
Chapter 11   *The Honeymoon Years* 67
Chapter 12   *Traveling, Todd, Tragedy, and Triumph* 75
Chapter 13   *Saint Joan* 81
Chapter 14   *Ministry Memories* 89
Chapter 15   *Four Months in Bed - My Miracle in Progress* 101
Chapter 16   *Jacklyn -The Little Missionary* 111
Chapter 17   *Jessica Danielle -Energy in Motion* 123
Chapter 18   *Ericka Jane -Parenting 101* 131
Chapter 19   *Losing Daddy? - Gaining a Miracle* 137
Chapter 20   *My Hero* 141
Chapter 21   *Funny Memories - Vacation Milestones* 147
Chapter 22   *Memory Makers and Milestone Builders* 157
Chapter 23   *Memories in the Making* 165
Epilogue   *Milestones Compiled* 169

FOREWORD

There is nothing more powerful than a personal testimony. You can argue doctrine, you can squabble over denominational differences, and even be at odds over Biblical interpretation...but no one can dispute a person's genuine encounter with God. A Christian's vital relationship with Jesus stands alone. That's why I thoroughly enjoy hearing or reading someone's autobiography and why I was honored to write the foreword to *Memories & Milestones.*

I have had the privilege of knowing Rick and Jennifer Pasquale for over 12 years. We have joined forces on several international church planting crusades, and have seen thousands of men, women and children give their lives to Christ. Whenever there was a tough missions project to tackle, I could always depend on the Pasquales. They're soldiers and won't flinch in the heat of the battle.

Memories & Milestones is an adventure. It is a journey through life. This book will move you emotionally and stir you spiritually. It has something for everyone. You will travel with Jennifer through her childhood, adolescence, teenage years and adulthood. You will laugh and you will cry.

You will stand with Jennifer in a hospital intensive care unit as she watched her mother die - tragically killed by a drunken driver. Her mother was only 39, Jennifer was 15. You'll weather the difficult years that followed and rejoice as Jennifer discovered God's perfect plan for her life.

From becoming the wife of Rick Pasquale, giving birth to their beautiful children, and now raising them in the admonition of the Lord, you can't help but cross paths, and find yourself as her story unfolds.

Someone once said, *"We are all in the school of God - and no one graduates."* Jennifer Pasquale is still enrolled. Only God knows what's in store.

Once again, this book is an adventure...because life is an adventure. So take the time, sit down and find yourself in the pages of this precious manuscript.

—Stephen Hill,
Missionary Evangelist,
currently at the Brownsville Revival in Pensacola, Florida

PROLOGUE

Deuteronomy 32:7 says, *"Remember the days of old, consider the years of many generations: ask thy father, and he will shew thee; thy elders and they will tell thee."*

This book is written to give glory and honor to God for bringing us through the past, walking with us today, and guiding our footsteps for tomorrow. It is important to recognize those people who have contributed to the person that we are becoming. It is a testimony of God's faithfulness, through mountain and valley experiences. One day, we will no longer look through the mirror of life with a distorted perspective. One day, we will stand face to Face with the One who "created us in His own image", and we will see the completion of His creation. We will be "His masterpiece". May all of our memories and milestones, be events that draw us closer to our Creator.

This book is especially dedicated to three very important people in my life. Without them, I would not be here to write it.

First, my precious mother, Jacklyn Jane Schaffer Jones, who went to be with the Lord in 1975. She gave me the best start in life any girl could ever hope for. She was my best friend.

Second, my wonderful father, Herbert Luther Jones. He also gave me life, and continues to be a constant source of encouragement and love. His example to me for the past thirty-six and one half years has continually drawn me closer to the Lord and given me an overwhelming appreciation for a Godly family.

And last, but in no way, least, my most precious grandmother, Alice Jane Schaffer Blythe. She has lived a life of unprecedented faithfulness to God, her family, and thousands of people around the globe. There are no words to describe how she has impacted my life and kept me going in the "paths of righteousness". At 82, she can still work, preach, give, and shop circles around me. She is incredible. To all three of these "joys of my life", I say, Thank you for the memories! Remembering has been sweet. I am richer because of your investments in me. I want this book to be an investment in the lives of all who read it, and may the returns be appreciated for eternity.

Found on the flyleaf of my mother's Bible:

*"Tomorrow begins today,
Today had its roots in yesterday,
The roots of yesterday determine tomorrow's tree."*

CHAPTER 1

Survival 101

The first memory I have is of my daddy. He was young, tall (especially from a 4 year old's perspective), blonde and very strong and he picked me up and threw me into our apartment swimming pool. "Daddy, don't throw her in. She can't swim", I wailed, as he threw our little black poodle, Cherie, into the deep blue. "It's OK", Daddy said, "she'll have to learn now." And the next thing I knew, he was throwing me in right behind her. "It's OK, Jen, swim, you can do it!" As I watched my little black ball of fur, doggie paddle to the steps, I did the same. I made it to the side and climbed up the ladder. Successful at my first lesson in independence.

Little did I know that I would have to learn how to do it by myself many more times and much earlier than most. Just like being tossed in that pool and THEN learning to swim, it seems my life has been full of lessons learned after the fact.

It would have been nice to have a calm, quiet lesson on the side of the pool and then gently slip into the water an inch at a time. But that's not life - at least not mine. It seems I've always jumped or been pushed in over my head and had to "doggie paddle" like crazy to keep afloat. Ever feel that way?

But just like that day when I knew my daddy was there to make sure I was OK and he wasn't going to let me drown, my (our) heavenly Father is always there making sure we're OK and He's holding out the Life Preserver (the Word) to keep us afloat. This book is about those memories of life, the milestones, and the One who always oversees every memory and christens every milestone.

Memory:

Born in Nashville, Tennessee on December 12, 1959, my parents and I moved to Texas six weeks later. I've been a TEXAN ever since. As far back as I can remember, I loved playing with my dolls, pretending to be a mommy, playing church and taking my "babies" right into church with me. I would pretend that all the other musicians were out sick and they would come and ask me to fill in at the piano. Sometimes, I'd even share a "testimony". It's not surprising that what we pretend as children, we now practice as adults.

Milestone:

A life's calling was being formed in the mind of a child and stimulated by those who had opportunity to influence her life.

CHAPTER 2

The Foundational Years

The first fourteen years of my life were mostly uneventful in my memory. But a lot of milestones were being formed and ready for placement. Like the ones made up of Mother and Daddy's love, their strict and involved guidance, family nights every Friday, and lots of talks around the kitchen table. What was it building? Love, trust, respect, openness, value structure, a sense of family and even more, which I've yet to realize.

I do realize that in this society, memories of family time, with two parents in the same home, is an obscure concept. However, it is a concept which God originated, ordained, and can still accomplish. A concept and life style that kept me close to the heart of God.

Memory:
During the 60's and 70's, it was not as common for a mother to work outside the home. But mine did. She was a Regional Executive Administrator for the Drug Enforcement Agency in Houston. She oversaw the funds for Federal Drug Agents making drug busts in 5 states. She was busy, but

never too busy. I never felt abandoned. Why? Because she was there at every important event in my life. She included me in her life by taking me to her office, introducing me to her co-workers, showing me the *Seized Property*, and always taking my calls. Even my routine orthodontist appointments became special, because those were our "out to lunch" days and special times alone together. Daddy worked faithfully, but my weekend memories always include him. If it was yard work, it was special to be "Daddy's helper", even though I'm sure it made the work take twice as long. I can't remember going to church without Daddy in the driver's seat, Mother in her seat, and me and brother Michael in the back (yes, fighting over who had more room). I'm sure they must have had one or two times out without us, but I don't remember being without them.

Milestone:
STABILITY

I would later realize how much I needed those stones of stability, love, values and trust. When your world is ripped apart on the outside, you only have what's left on the inside to get you through. Thank goodness, Mother and Daddy were making deposits in my emotional bank. Deposits that I would later draw from, often. Did they know what they were doing? Did they consciously realize the importance of those Saturday morning pancake breakfasts? Was it mundane or demanding at times? Maybe so, but they chose to give me the gift of life and they knew it was a gift that keeps on giving. The rewards and responsibilities went hand in hand, one outweighing the other many times, I'm sure. Unknowingly, perhaps, they were giving me precious moments to remember. The gift of memories unwrapped bringing joy, understanding and acceptance. Unwrapped for their children, to be later passed on to mine. By looking back, I can step forward with a strong emotional and spiritual backup, sometimes forgotten in the busyness of moving ahead. Memories that became milestones.

CHAPTER 3

What is a Memory?

What is a memory? A memory is special. It impacts our thought process because it is forever logged in the mind's data bank. It is something significant, that brings with it a more intense feeling of emotion than the average. A memory is a recollection of a past event, person or emotion. Granted, some memories can be distorted or changed by verbal suggestion or outside influences, but that's another book. We'll leave that to the clinical psychologist, I have yet to become. The memories I'm referring to are those in the heart as well as in the mind.

Some of my memories are:
* My birthday party at a local amusement park, lots of friends, about 7 years old
* Horseback riding, double, with my brother, then getting bucked off as we approached the stable, about 10 years old
* Dancing with my Daddy, me on his feet, to Hee Haw on TV, in the family room, probably 6 years old
* Going to Papaw's and eating out in the long kitchen, behind the double swinging doors
* My first kiss, he said I kissed like a rocking chair (I still don't know what that means), 15 years old
* My first beauty salon haircut AND style, 13 years old

* Services at church camp, Boy, was God Cool! - 11, 12, 13, 14 years old

Were all these memories milestones? No, but they did affect me then and I do remember them now. We can't deny the past's effect on our lives today. If your past was bad, be thankful you made it through. If it was good, share it with someone and give them the hope that dreams can be fulfilled.

I could share so many others. I remember spankings, followed by "I Love You" lectures. (I knew it was correction, I knew it was love, it WAS keeping me on the right path.) I remember shopping trips, vacations to Grandma's, celebrating Christmas with the silver aluminum tree with red shiny balls (I used it for the first two years of my marriage. Imagine what it looked like after 20 years, crinkled aluminum foil). I remember summers on the beach, boiled shrimp from Galveston, boiled skin (sunburn) from the hot Texas sun. I remember my pastor, my youth pastor, their wives, their children, Mrs. Rice - my first grade Sunday School teacher, Coach Miller, my 7th grade math teacher, Kathy Tinnin, my mom's best friend and my wedding coordinator, my friend "Mousie" otherwise known as Janet, my own nickname "Safari Lady" - all because of a souvenir necklace I wore one time.

Is it good to remember? Yes. Do you remember? Think back, perhaps certain seasons of life stick out in your mind. Ecclesiastes says, *"To everything there is a season, and a time to every purpose under the heaven: A time to be born, and a time to die: a time to plant, and a time to harvest; a time to kill, and a time to heal; a time to break down, and a time to build up; a time to laugh, a time to cry, a time to mourn and a time to dance......"*

So yes, memories are part of life's process, part of growth. Dick Foth once said, "Remembering causes appreciation for life with all of it's ebbs and flows intensified." When I look back, I see, really see, how far I have come. Who would have thought? Not me, maybe not you. But God knew. God begins a work for us on the day of our conception. Jeremiah says, *"Before I formed thee in the belly, I knew thee; and before thou camest forth out of the womb, I sanctified thee."*

There's another memory. A memory of stories told, passages read. It's a memory of an old rugged cross and a crown of thorns. In order to see God in my life, I must look back in His life as well. Without the memory of the cross, there would be no hope for eternity, no reason to look ahead. There was suffering in His past. There was the time He felt *alone* when He got lost in the crowd as a boy. He felt *frustrated* when His closest friends doubted his abilities. He was *angry* when strangers made a mockery of His Father's house. He *wept* at the death of His good friend, even though He would later perform a miracle in the same situation. (We don't always see the miraculous possibilities, only the crisis at the moment). I'm sure He felt *rushed* to feed the 5,000 and distribute all that food with so little to work with. He felt *betrayed* by Judas. He felt *joy* when Mary anointed His feet to show Him her love. He felt *satisfaction* in forgiving the woman caught in adultery and teaching the Pharisees a lesson on hypocrisy at the same time. He felt *abandoned* on the cross. He felt *peace* at the end. He felt it all. And He did it for you and me.

There is comfort in knowing. Comfort in the fact that someone does understand. Someone does rejoice with me, pleads for me to the Father. I am not alone. I remember.

Memories - precious moments - possible milestones - definitely stepping stones.

CHAPTER 4

Remembering Momma

My mother was born in 1936 in Colorado. She was born into the home of Rev. Jacob and Rev. Jane Schaffer. A preacher's kid. A year and a half later, her sister, Joyce, was born. They would be best friends. Mother was the typical first born; more serious, more structured, more "prissy". Aunt Joyce was the baby; more silly, more carefree, more "tomboy".

I remember them telling me about the time when they were just 4 years and 3 years old and Mother was afraid of cats. Joyce found a cat in the back yard and wrapped her little arms around it and picked it up. The cat was as long as she was. With it's legs dragging the ground, Joyce ran around that backyard, chasing Jacklyn with the cat, Joyce laughing and giggling and Jacklyn screaming and crying.

Another time, when they were in their teens, they told me how Mother was on the phone to a very special boy and she had just done her hair to go out. Joyce came along and put both hands in Mother's hair and just messed it all up. Jacklyn, who was drying a large, tin platter at the time, just took that platter and whacked Joyce right over the head. Needless, to say the phone call was ended, by Grandma, I'm sure.

Another memory they shared with me, was of times when one or the other was sick. They would always be there to support each other. After they were married, both of them had various surgeries they had to undergo. When Joyce had her mastectomy, Mother took a leave from her job in Houston, flew to Nashville, and stayed with Joyce until she was better. When Mother had a hysterectomy, Joyce left her job, flew to Houston, and stayed until Mother was back on her feet.

Mother had two children, me (d.o.b. 12/12/59) and Michael (d.o.b. 4/1/65). Mother did have a funny bone, too. When Michael was born, my dad really wanted a boy. In those days, the husband didn't get to be in the delivery room. When Michael was born on April Fool's day, Mother thought it would be funny to wrap him up in a pink blanket and tell Daddy it was a girl. The nurses brought Mother out of the recovery room in a wheel chair, holding this precious little bundle of pink. My dad tried to appear happy, as he kissed Mother, and just as he leaned down to kiss the baby, she pulled back the blanket to reveal a wonderfully naked, baby boy, and said, "April fool's!" They said my dad was so excited and laughing and crying at the same time. Aren't surprises fun?

As I've already discussed, Mother was a working mom. She was very intelligent and very organized. She was well known in government agency circles as a woman who could organize any office. She did not graduate from college, but she always pursued new horizons. She would take us to the symphony, operas, Rodeos, the circus, the Ice Capades, the beach, the library, church events, snow skiing (not in Texas), and anything else to keep our perspective on life broad, well informed and rich in texture. She was wonderful!

Mother was very classy too. She loved beautiful, quality clothes. But, she was also a good steward; however, not a seamstress. Therefore, she would buy material and patterns and have a seamstress make her something that she had seen in a magazine. She was raised in a preacher's home, where make up was not worn. But, even without make up, she was always beautiful. I remember when I was about 13, she was ready to let me start wearing make up. She didn't know how to teach me, so she enrolled me in a modeling class at our local department store. She learned along with me. She bought some make up too and we were so proud, she and I.

Memory:
My mother knew a lot about everything, but always wanted to learn more, and she never acted prideful. She loved talking to all kinds of people and would help anybody, any time.

Milestone:
She was teaching me, through her example, that you can always improve, and still be a good steward of the talents and gifts God gives.

I found this old newspaper clipping in Mother's bible:

What I Want My Children to Remember About Home...
(author unknown)
THAT their father and mother loved each other.
THAT the reason home was a happy one was because we all worked to keep it so.
THAT each child was given every possible opportunity to develop his own personality.
THAT each child's personal possessions were inviolable if kept in the place allotted to them.
THAT the books in the house were to be read if handled rightly, and there were no shelves under lock and key because of questionable contents.
THAT absolute truth abode there; no earnest questioner, how-

ever young, was put off with subterfuge or evasion.

THAT we believed in hospitality in spite of any extra labor involved, and that our friends loved to come to us.

THAT Sunday was the happiest day in the week and that we all looked forward to its coming because it was the day when we went to Church together, then came home for an afternoon with father in the midst.

THAT though father and mother worked hard and long at their respective jobs, they found time every day to keep informed on current events, to read good books, to think things through to logical conclusions and to PRAY.

This is definitely what I remember about Momma.

CHAPTER 5

The Car Wreck

The summer of 1975. Mother was 39 years old. She and Daddy would celebrate 21 years of marriage in December. I was 15 and Michael was 10. School was out and it was time for summer fun. June, 1975 will forever be engraved in the transcript of my life. With the exception of a few, very painful days, subconsciously locked away, it is a summer I remember in vivid detail. The exact days and times all run together, but the events are plain.

It started with an invitation from my friend, Robin and her family, to spend some time with them at a condo on the beach. (Definitely a milestone - because I accepted that invitation, I am here today) I remember calling my mother on the phone at work to say good bye. "Be sweet", she said. "Remember your manners. Have fun. I love you." "I love you, too, Momma". The last words spoken.

Milestone:
It's important to choose all of our words carefully. You never know if they will be your last, or the last for someone else to hear.

I remember being at the condo and talking to Robin about my mother. I wanted to be a better child, wanted to accept her guidance and honor her wishes with regard to a person I was dating. I wanted to tell her I was sorry for being so stubborn lately. I wanted to tell her she was the best. "You'll get to, Jennifer." Robin said. But I never did.

It was going on 3:00 in the morning, and I had been crying for hours. Robin didn't understand, but she was praying with me. I didn't understand, but I think God was getting me ready. Suddenly, there was a knock on the condo door. It was a beach patrol, who had been looking for a girl named Jennifer Jones, staying with the Sanders family. (There was no phone in the condo and my parents didn't know the exact beach address). I knew immediately it was for me. He told us there had been an accident and my parents and my brother were in the hospital and it didn't look hopeful for my mother. Robin's parents, Robin and I got dressed and they drove me back to Houston to the hospital where we thought they had all been taken. It was a two hour drive which I do not remember.

When we arrived at the hospital, they took me to my father's room. I was not prepared for what I saw. My dad and my brother, Michael, were in the same room, in separate beds. My dad had his whole head wrapped in gauze and cuts on his face and hands. Michael had his leg in a cast and over 100 stitches in his head and face. I later learned that my dad's ear had been cut off, and a wonderful plastic surgeon had reattached it.

I remember asking "What happened? Where's Momma?" My parents and Michael had gone out for a family night. On the way home, on a dark, country, Texas road, a drunk driver had come speeding out of nowhere, just as they approached an intersection. He had no headlights on as he broadsided their two month old, Bronze, Chrysler LeBaron at about 60 - 70 mph, crashing into Mother's side of the car, causing the car to look like it had folded in half with barely room for one person between the two sides. Michael always sat behind Daddy, and I always sat behind Mother. There was nothing left of the right side.

Mother had extensive brain and internal injuries and had been taken to the Ben Taub Trauma Hospital in downtown Houston, while Michael and Daddy had been taken to the nearest suburban hospital. They never saw Mother again.

After holding my dad and brother and being reassured by doctors, nurses, and friends that they were OK, Robin's parents took me downtown to see Mother.

When we arrived, my grandparents were just getting in from Tennessee. The nurses in Intensive Care were not going to let me in, because I was only 15 and you had to be 18. My grandmother insisted that they let me see her, as we all knew this might be my only chance to say good-bye.

It didn't seem like it was Mother laying there. Her head was swollen to twice it's normal size, her eyes were swollen as big as baseballs and extremely black and purple. She had tubes and machines hooked up everywhere. Her lips were in a pursed, kind of biting position as if she was trying to be brave and endure. The nurse told me she couldn't hear me, but it was OK to touch her. I remember looking at the machines and seeing brain waves and heart rhythms. I was so afraid to touch her because it looked like every part of her must be in terrible pain. I remember reaching down and touching her hand, whispering , "I Love You Momma", over and over and over. She had always been there to take care of my problems and there was nothing I could do to take care of this problem. It was an overwhelmingly desperate feeling. Finally, the nurse asked me to leave and all I could do was just cry in my grandmother's arms.

For the next two days, I stayed mostly at the other hospital with Michael and Daddy. I remember sitting in the hallway outside their room as people, friends, pastors, medical staff, came and went.

I had a wonderful friend in my life at that time, named John. He was with me through the whole thing. He loved Mother. She had chaperoned several youth events and spent some time praying with him, trying to encourage him to give 100% to the Lord. He was the one I knew she did not want me to get too close to and yet there was no one else for me at that moment.

On the third day, John was driving me downtown to see Mother again. "She is going to make it Jennifer", he said, "I know she's strong and she'll pull through." But, something inside me knew this was not going to be. "No", I said, "I'm going to say good-bye today". When I walked into the intensive care this time, I noticed that even though all the same machines and tubes were still there, every machine had a straight line going across it. No brain activity, no heart rhythms, only the sound of the breathing machine taking the breaths. Her lips were no longer pursed together the way they had been. It was as if she was already at peace, somewhere else. I think I said a few more words this time, told her I loved her and that she was the best mother, and then I kissed her on the cheek, said good bye, let my hand glide softly across the top of her hand and silently walked out into the hallway.

Milestone:
The stability of the past, was now keeping me stable in a supernatural way. I was losing one of the most precious gifts ever given to me and gaining another one at the same time, TRUST in the Giver of Gifts.

It would be just a few hours later when Grandma and Papa would be told that Mother had passed away. They would leave Ben Taub and go to the other hospital to tell us she was gone. On their way out of the hospital, as they passed through the lobby, the grief of losing their daughter overwhelming, down, but not defeated! Grandma spotted a young couple sitting, not too close to one another, but on the same bench and crying. She went over to them, and said, "I am a minister, you look like you are hurting, Can I pray for you?" The couple explained that their three year old daughter was upstairs in intensive care and she was dying. They were overwhelmed with hopelessness. Grandma told them, "I've just lost my baby girl, she was thirty nine years old. But I know God can heal your daughter." And so, out of her grief, she reached out in faith for this young couple and their child. Weeks later, we found out that the couple's child had been miraculously healed, they had been on the verge of divorce, and had gone to a Baptist church and rededicated their lives to the Lord and each other. God had done a miracle for them because Grandma had looked past her tragedy and stepped into their miracle. Now that's a milestone!

Milestone:
Even in the midst of your most tragic moment, there will be someone else who needs a word of hope. As we express hope to others, our own sense of overwhelming difficulty can serve as a reminder of His overwhelming ability to come through in the crisis. God is able! Someone once said, "If He can make a man out of a ball of mud, if He can make a highway through the River Jordan, if He can make a taxi out of a whale, if He can make wine from water, if He can make a banquet out of a boy's lunch, if He can make blind eyes see, deaf ears hear, the lame walk and the dead live, then HE IS ABLE to be there for me in my hour of need. TRUST and share that trust!

I was then taken back to Daddy's hospital. I remember them putting Michael in the same bed with Daddy. My youth pastor, Mike Cave was there, our pastor, Bro. Robert Goree, mother's friend, Kathy Tinnin, John and Grandma and Papa, and maybe others, but I don't remember. I held onto someone as Pastor Goree told us that Mother had quit breathing sometime that evening and she was now with the Lord. I can not describe the tears, the pain on the inside of my stomach. Daddy sobbing, Michael sobbing, everyone crying. Kathy holding me, John holding me, Mike Cave holding me, but not Mother. She would never hold me again. My world had been shattered and my heart shattered right along with it.

The next few days of funeral preparations are not in my mind. I know that family was flying in from all over. Regena, mother's co-worker at DEA, was helping to make the arrangements and meeting with Daddy and our grandparents in the hospital.

Mother wanted and needed a closed casket, so Regena had a very beautiful picture of her at work, blown up and beautifully framed to sit on top of the casket.

I'm sure I slept at home, but I don't remember. Daddy and Michael were dismissed from the hospital in time to go to the funeral.

I hated riding in the back of that big, black limousine. It was the darkest day of my life.

I remember Daddy sobbing so hard at the funeral home that I thought he would die too. The place was packed with friends and co-workers, DEA agents, family and former pastors and neighbors as well. Mother had made a tremendous impact on people's lives and they were coming out of respect to her, but also in support of us. I felt that support.

When we arrived at the cemetery, my foot fell asleep as we got out of the limo and I almost fell down. Maybe it wasn't just my foot, I don't remember. I do remember Robin and her parents being right there to hold me up. I hadn't got to see them since they had first dropped me off at the hospital. It meant so much to me just to see them standing there for me.

I don't know who I held on to. I think I held on to my cousin, Cande. My grandparents were supporting Daddy and someone was carrying Michael.

The details of the memory aren't as important as the memory itself. I need to remember that terrible dark day, because I was not alone. As I look back, I see how many people were helping us get through this. And I realize how important just being there is.

Milestone:
Sometimes, I think we feel useless in others tragedies, therefore we do not allow ourselves to be used. But, just being there speaks even louder than words sometimes. Dependability - horizontally and vertically; I must recognize, that between God and me, we can depend on each other, and I must also recognize, that between me and others, we can depend on each other.

Milestone:
To cry, showing a continued sensitivity. Not putting up a tough exterior. Remember, what you pretend, you later practice. A conscious decision to continue to trust God, not blame Him; to allow others to be in my life - this would be a character trait blossoming for the future.

There were other very important people too. Mary Hulet, our live-in Nanny and House Keeper. In fact, by the mercy of God and for some unknown reason, the very day of the accident, Mother had just sat down with Mary, giving her all of the out of town family's phone numbers and other pertinent information, in case of an emergency. Mary made many of the initial phone calls. She was a wonderful Christian widow who was so patient, and kind during the next few weeks. She kept us going. She's receiving her reward along with Mother, now. All of our friends, neighbors, family. I remember, there was so much food and so many people around, constantly.

I remember after the funeral, we were back at home and the phone rang. I ran to get it, forgetting that Mother would not be on the other end as she had so often when calling from work. I felt so devastated to hear someone else's voice on the other end. I don't remember who it was, but I remember, I didn't want to answer the phone any more for a while.

I also remember being back in church several weeks later. I was sitting on the far side and I was sure I had seen Mother standing in the foyer. I got up and ran around to the foyer. I looked in the bathroom. I ran outside and looked in the parking lot. Everything was quiet and empty. I knew I had seen her with her beautiful, black hair, standing there, but there was no one. I remember walking back into the building as if I had just lost her again.

Milestone:

The realization that she was gone, and making the choice to begin to step forward, one stone at a time.

CHAPTER 6

What is a Milestone?

Milestones are turning points in our life. After each milestone, our life takes on a new dimension, sometimes a new direction.

Milestones sometimes feel like millstones around our neck. But the CORNERSTONE keeps us upright.

A memory is special but a milestone is work.

A milestone is made up of many emotional miles.

A milestone affects me, memories were affected by others.

Something you KNOW - this is a milestone.

Memories give us the tools and equipment we use to lay the foundation for the milestone.

Milestones build our tomorrows.

Memories affect today, milestones affect tomorrow.

Memories fade with time, milestones are never forgotten.

Memories can be captured on camera, milestones are captured by the heart.

The memory says lonely, the milestone says not lost.

The memory says down, the milestone says not deserted.

The memory says bewildered, the milestone says still believing.

The memory says happy, the milestone says contented.

CHAPTER 7

Changes

After Mother died, my whole life changed. My dad sold the house and moved into a town house. Michael and I went to live with Aunt Joyce for a year, because Daddy was traveling off shore a lot and couldn't be home with us. I finally broke up with John, because he just wasn't strong in the Lord and I needed strength.

I left high school after my junior year to go to college as an advanced placement student. But I really did it to put the past behind and begin a new, happier, chapter in my life. It took a while for me to realize that I could dream again. My expectations were low. I thought something bad would happen again. I thought I would have to settle for second best because my perfect life was no longer perfect. BUT, God always exceeds our expectations, even if we don't have any.

I couldn't expect very much from Daddy at this time. He was in tremendous grief. His mother died six months later. It was a very hard year. The first thing that needed changing, was my attitude towards Daddy. I couldn't understand why he had to sell our house and get rid of ALL Mother's things. (Luckily, Regena was still in the picture and while she was helping Daddy move things out, she was SAVING them for me and Michael. Daddy would appreciate it later, I know I did.)

Michael and I had gone to spend the remainder of the summer with Grandma and Papa Schaffer (Mother's parents) in Sweetwater, Tennessee. Before we left, it seemed that everything I did made Daddy upset. I missed Mother so bad, and yet he missed her too. Consequently, we weren't any consolation for each other at that time.

While in Tennesse, I went to a Tent Crusade. I remember thinking, "I hope the evangelist doesn't try to pray for me". I guess I was still trying to console myself, rather than letting the Holy Spirit comfort me as I should. But, the Lord had other plans.

I was praying with my eyes shut, angry at my Dad for not being able to take care of me at this time. I needed him and it felt like he was pushing me away. I thought my way of handling our loss was the best, and Daddy was definitely not grieving with me. I guess I almost felt like I didn't care if I ever saw him again. I had physically lost one parent and emotionally lost the other. Boy, was I mad. Hatred was trying to infiltrate me. As I was praying, (if you call it that.) with my eyes shut, so the evangelist wouldn't look at me, he must have looked at me anyway. I felt him walking closer. I could feel his breath as he was praying out loud. I could smell his cologne. I knew he was about to pray for me.

Milestone:
When God grabs hold of your life, He NEVER lets go. Even if you try to loosen your grip, He's still holding on.

Anyway, under the anointing of the Holy Spirit, the evangelist began to lay his hands on my shoulder. He was interceding for me. He was speaking a word of knowledge into my face. He said something like, "You have lost something very important to you, you are very bitter about this and you are taking your bitterness out on those you love. God wants to remove the bitterness and fill the void with His love and understanding." About that time, I fell down under the power of God. As I was laying there, I began to feel, literally feel, God's hand scooping out ALL of the pain, anger, hatred, bitterness, and grief. I felt as though He was scooping out my heart, and suddenly, it was as if 1,000 pounds was lifted off my chest. The burden was being lifted. Then, I felt, literally felt, God pouring love, unconditional love and supernatural understanding into the crater of my heart that had been made by the grief. It was as if I could see God's hand, holding a huge pitcher, and liquid love was pouring out of the pitcher into my heart. I felt it spill over, out of my heart, into my blood stream. I could feel it coursing through my veins, all the way from my head down to my toes and back through my heart again. It was like a saturation of my blood stream, a saturation of the presence of God, filling the void in my life. I was getting a new heart. Ezekial 36:26 says, *"A new heart also will I give you, and a new spirit will I put within you: and I will take away the stony heart out of your flesh,.. and I will put my spirit within you."*

When I finally did get up, I LOVED my Daddy! It was God's love, *agape*. I could not wait to get home and call him on the phone. I wanted to tell him I was sorry I had not comforted him. I had not tried to realize what it must be like to lose your best friend of twenty years, literally the other part of yourself. I had been selfish and I wanted to hold my Daddy, hug him and grieve with him. *God was restoring my joy and it was time to share the restoration with my family.*

I can honestly say, that it was at that moment, that God gave me a sensitivity to people that helps me in ministry, today. It was as if I had just had a spiritual and emotional surgery. And, along with the surgery, there is always the recovery time. And even, after the recovery, there are usually several weeks of rehabilitation. Learning to live with the postsurgical condition. I was learning to live without my mother. I was learning to live in a single - parent household. It was unrealistic of me, to expect things to keep operating the way they had prior to Mother's death. When circumstances change, we have to be flexible, pliable in the Sculptor's hands, for modifications. This does not just happen with tragedies in our lives, but with a variety of changing circumstances in an ever changing society. Are we constantly making the effort to be pliable in the Lord's hand?

There is another little poem in Mother's bible that goes like this:

> "God, grant me the serenity to accept the things
> I cannot change,
> The courage to change the things I can,
> And the wisdom to know the difference."

The next change to take place shortly after Mother's death, was Daddy's marriage to Regena. (you remember, Mother's co-worker at DEA). They had opportunities to be together, following the funeral, because Regena was so helpful in closing Mother's office and packing up her things. She had also taken the casket picture of Mother and had several copies beautifully matted and framed for members of the family. So, they would sometimes grab a bite to eat, after the "business" was taken care of. Eventually, they fell in love. I take pride in knowing that, according to Regena, she actually fell in love with Daddy's children first.

I will admit, I was not very happy when I realized my dad was going to remarry, just one year after Mother's death. However, I had a wonderful youth pastor's wife who helped me to realize that Mother and Daddy must have had a wonderful marriage, and that Daddy must have enjoyed being married so much, that he wanted to do it again, soon. I also realize, now, the he needed a companion, someone to share his life and the life of his children with. (It's funny, some things you don't realize or appreciate until you have been there yourself. I definitely appreciate the spousal relationship and inner dynamics much more, now that I've had my own spouse for 18 years.)

I did not want to be a part of the national statistics of children with stepparents. However, the memory was in the making. I had friends that were part of divorced homes, with stepparents. They had not painted a pretty picture of that life. There were not too many books on "Blended Families". Regena had no children, so how would she know what to do with me and Michael? What would happen to our maternal grandparents? Who would we share holidays with? But with God, the details always work out. The definition of IDEAL is often redefined, but the definition of LOVE is unchanging. We still had love, all of us.

Milestone:
The picture doesn't have to be perfect to be enjoyed. It's life's imperfections that make us appreciate the beauty. If we didn't have winter, with all it's gray, cold, and dreary days, and all the bare branches, we would never appreciate the fresh spring breeze, the newly blossoming plants, the new growth and the old growth being revived. That's what happens with change. New growth in some areas. Other areas just get revived with time. Time does heal.

Looking back, I also see how important it is to recognize children's unspoken fears and concerns. Michael didn't express some of those feelings for three years. As I already stated, my brother, Michael, was in the car and injured severely. It was three years before he finally expressed to Rick, whom I had just begun dating, that he thought the accident was his fault. He thought that if he had been awake in the back seat, he could have seen the car coming and warned my parents. Of course, this wouldn't have happened, because it was a pitch black, back country road, and the drunk driver was driving with no headlights on at high speed.

Children often do not know how to express their insecurities. Instead they act out or, as in Michael's case, just withdraw. It was the love within our family that brought Michael out of his guilt and helped him to feel safe enough to express it, even if it was to an "outsider". I will always be thankful that the "college boy" Rick took time with the "little elementary, brother", to begin to build trust. It's important to make every opportunity for families to *blend* together.

Before I close this chapter on change, I do want to recognize how Regena changed my/our lives for the better. There's always two sides to every road. Some might feel, (Michael and I, both, probably felt at some point,) that it would be better not to remarry, at least, not so soon. We could have had Daddy all to ourselves. I was 15 years old. I could have cooked dinners and helped with household duties. However, Daddy did not bring Regena into our lives to do chores. She brought life back to our house.

When I tried to rebel and run away, she was there, and because she was neutral, I felt I could run to her and she would listen to my side. She did, too. She never failed to have "pillow talk" with me after my dates. She helped me find my "dream" wedding dress and still stay within the budget Daddy had given me (even though, it probably put hundreds of miles on her car). She found Mother's diary of her pre-wedding night and gave it to me on my pre-wedding night, so that I would feel like Mother was still sharing the day with me. She stayed up many nights making things for me and probably praying for me, too. Even though, I did not have Mother, her *successor*, covered all the bases.

She was the kind of Stepmother you never read about. One that was not jealous of the previous wife. In fact, she loved her too. She shared memories with us and allowed us the freedom to constantly and joyfully remember Mother. What a gift Regena has been to our family.

Regena and Daddy, together, also gave Michael and me another gift. Tiffanie Rachelle. Talk about changes!! It had been eleven years since there was a baby in the house. But, the minute the doctor wheeled that little red faced, blonde haired baby out to the window, we were a family again. It was no longer his or hers, it was ours.

Tiffanie definitely had to pay her dues, however. Her first room was a closet with a window, converted to a nursery, in the Master bedroom of the town house they had moved to. (She's made up for it since. She was practically an only child and had Daddy all to herself. She was spoiled by all, but it never spoiled her character. She is a wonderful sister.)

Milestone:
Anyone can contribute to a family, if given the opportunity. I'm thankful that I had mentors in my life encouraging me to give Regena a chance. To appreciate the value of BLENDING. Consequently, Regena encouraged my emotional growth, and helped me to continue improving my life skills.

CHAPTER 8

Daddy

Every step forward I have ever taken, has been influenced by Herbert L. Jones, the one who gave me life and almost took it away on that day at the swimming pool when I was four (or so I thought at the time.) Truly, I have learned so many valuable lessons in watching Daddy grow. Parents grow too, you know.

Herbert L. Jones was born in 1935 in Kennett, Missouri. His parents, Papaw and Mama Nez were farmers. Daddy was the youngest of three, with two older sisters.

He and Mother met in High School when she dropped her books. He offered to pick them up, and she, very independently, replied, "Thank you, I can do it." (I think Mother was just trying to play hard to get. It worked!) Daddy, known as "Sonny" to all those who had watched him grow, was always the perfect gentleman. He learned from a young age, that you have to work hard to get ahead and he has always worked hard to give his best to all of his family.

Memory:
Even after, he was married, with a family, he was still pursuing his education and ultimately graduated with a Degree in Engineering from the University of Houston. Daddy worked

for several companies over the years. First, in my memory, was Southern Pacific. I used to think because he was an engineer, that he was the one driving the train. He wasn't that kind of engineer. He was a civil engineer, and later a structural engineer, too. He worked for Texaco most of my growing up years, and then transferred to Conoco, after Mother's death, I think.

While with Conoco, he traveled to Alaska, England, Ireland and other places working on very important projects for oil drilling.

He worked on designing a template for the FIRST floating oil rig in the North Sea. He moved the family to California for this job. Unfortunately, I had already left home. I did get to visit them during their stay in London and also, Irvine, California. (My husband was always so good to make sure I kept my strong family ties.)

Then, he took early retirement from Conoco and opened a Speedy Printing business in Houston. He had to go to school for this too. Unfortunately, the printing shop was opened during a time when Houston was in a deep recession and the business did not last very long. But Daddy was resilient! He's always been a thinker, if it doesn't work one way, you find another way to solve it.

It took him a little while to get over the disappointment of losing the printing shop. But during that time, he saturated his mind with God's word, on tape, on video, on Christian radio. I firmly believe it was this continued "programming" of his mind that kept him moving forward.

Then, he went back to college to get his Teaching Certificate and taught Jr. High and Sr. High school for awhile.
A second "degree" and he was over fifty. He also did some free-lance engineering on the side. Wow, he's incredible!

Milestone:
You're never too old to get an education. Education is very important, even if you have to sacrifice to get it. AND, education is a life long pursuit.

Memory:
Daddy loved the outdoors. He was always working on the landscaping, designing things. He allowed us to have pets. More than one. He even tried to blend our pet family by bringing a kitten home to Cherie, our black poodle and Dutchess, our Great Dane. They could have probably worked out an arrangement, but remember, Mother never liked cats and the little kitten was gone in less than twelve hours. We had two horses that I remember. Carla, was a wild, semi-tame, mustang, named after Hurricane Carla (she's the one that bucked me and Michael off). Ginger, was a big mare, so gentle, that when Michael fell off the saddle, she just stopped and waited for someone to come help him. She also had a colt, who we sold or gave away, I don't remember. (Memories are selective at times.)

Milestone:
A love for nature and all of God's creation. We now have a St. Bernard in our household. I wonder if Mother would have approved? (Sometimes, it's hard when memories can't answer questions for today. It's like not having enough information in the data bank to gather a conclusion. It's like being thrown in and THEN learning to swim, you just have to do the best you can.)

Memory:

I remember so many wonderful times when I could talk to my Daddy. Especially, after my spiritual surgery, the rehabilitation was 100% effective.

Like the time when I came home and told Daddy that my boyfriend had caressed my breasts and what should I do? I think he almost had a heart attack, but he stayed calm. He told me that he understood how things can get out of control sometimes, how I had every right to say No, and that if my date did not respect me that He (Daddy) would take care of that. He let me know I should not let things go that far again, but never made me feel dirty or embarrassed. In fact, I had more courage to restrain the next time, because I knew my daddy would be there for me.

There was the other, very, significant moment, when my future husband, Rick, and I, came to talk to Daddy to ask permission to get married. I remember this one vividly.

Daddy was standing in the kitchen, getting ready to pour a glass of milk as he stood over the glass top, kitchen table. Rick and I walked in through the sliding glass door off the patio. Rick, usually Mr. Macho, always in control of every situation, nervously addressed my father, "Hi, Burt. (Rick was from the north and never learned to address your perspective father as Mr.) I would like to let you know that I've asked Jennifer to marry me, and I / we would like to have your blessing."

I thought the glass table would break as Daddy *abruptly* sat the glass of milk down and then sat himself down. "Well", Daddy replied, "I guess you better sit down here and tell me your plans. How exactly do you plan to support Jennifer? What will she do about continuing her college education? Where do you plan on living? etc., etc., etc."

Mr. Macho took over. Not really, but Rick definitely knew the direction the Lord would have us go and was able to express to Daddy how working for the Lord means being flexible in your plans.

It was the first of many discussions with Daddy about letting God lead and being ready to do whatever, or go wherever God Directs. It was the beginning (or maybe just the continuation) of a parent putting the child totally in the hands of God. We did have a plan, but it did change two months before the wedding.

After about an hour of discussion, however, Daddy gave us his blessing and said he was happy for us and loved us both. I think it was several years later, before his love for Rick was truly that of a *father to a son*. This, we understand much better now, too, after having three of our own daughters to worry over. Looking back, I can see that Daddy was truly a wonderful guardian of the children God had left him to raise alone.

Milestone:
I could always talk to my father. In the future, there would be so many times when the Lord would use my earthly father to give me HIS divine guidance. When I accept the wisdom of the one whom God has placed over me, I am accepting God's wisdom - the umbrella of authority is protecting me from the elements.

Memory:
My memories of Daddy, cause me to jump around in fragments of time. I remember missing Mother many times, only to have Daddy call, write, or send a little present, like a tape or some safety device, reminding me once again that I still have a parent who is there, even though miles away.

One time, I had to have surgery. I will write about that more, but my memory of Daddy is important to this chapter. I had to be in bed for two months after surgery and my husband was traveling. I knew if I had Mother, she would fly to Michigan and be with me, just like she had done for Aunt Joyce. So, I called Daddy. I said, "I need you. I can't do this recovery without you. There will be no one to take care of the girls, get their dinners, get them off to school, etc." Daddy said, "Well, I guess I could come, but I can't do their hair." I don't know any man who can or will do his daughter's hair, unless he's a hair stylist.

Anyway, the memory is that Daddy was there for me. He didn't miss a beat. He stayed with me for two weeks, doing laundry, dishes, dinner, doing the taxi bit for the girls, sitting with me when I was awake, and fixing things around the house. Every time I use my kitchen faucet, I remember. Daddy was there, he cared. However, he never did do the hair routine.

Milestone:
Two things stick out in my data bank here. One, my earthly family is very precious. The blessing of being able to be depended on is a precious gift to pass down for generations. The Italians are very big on this. (another chapter) Two, just like the kitchen faucet causes me to remember Daddy. God's word causes us to remember His faithfulness in our lives. He wants us to use it just as much as the kitchen faucet. And every time we touch it, it is serving a different purpose in our lives. And every time we touch it, the Word, it should serve as a reminder that our Heavenly Father is there, He cares, and He will always come through.

There is one more, very recent, memory of Daddy. It is so important, that it will receive an entire chapter, according to chronological happenings. Read on!

CHAPTER 9

Meeting "Mr. Right"

I've already mentioned that I broke up with John. But, in order to do that, the Lord intervened.

I was 16 years old, and it's the first time I remember really fasting and praying to seek God's will. I knew that John was not the one for me. I was beginning to feel my calling to the ministry, which he did not share. However, he had been with me through so much. We had been emotionally intimate and I did not know how I would do without him.

My youth group was getting ready to go on their annual Ski Retreat to Estes Park, Colorado. John and I were both going.

For one solid week, every time my parents set down to dinner, I would go to my bedroom and get down on my knees, beside my bed. I was seeking God. I told Him that I could not be without someone. I had a very low self-esteem and I thought if I gave up John, I would never have anyone else. We planned to get married when I was 18. I asked the Lord, to cause somebody else, somebody VERY good looking, to show interest in me. I didn't need another boyfriend, exactly, but just to know that I might be attractive to other guys. It was a very specific prayer.

After seven days, it was time to go to the retreat. On the bus ride there, I was with John. At the first service, there was a musical group from Southwestern Assemblies of God College. There was the most awesome Italian guy playing the trumpet AND worshipping God. Good looking and spiritual!

I told my chaperone, Brenda Powell, that I thought that guy was a Hunk (seventies term for great). Well, she took over from there. She told me to tell John that I was not feeling well and wanted to go to my room, (not exactly a lie, since I was feeling a little "love sick"). So, John dropped me off at my room and said good night. Then, Brenda took me back to the service room, where the band was doing a little "jammin". She saw him (Rick) in there, *pushed* me into the room, and said, "This girl wants to meet you." I could have died!

The Italian Stallion, ever cool, winked at me (Oh, what that wink still does to my heart!), told us they were going out to eat and would be back in an hour. "If you want to play cards, meet us down the hall in an hour. Do you know how to play cards?" Rick's first words to me. I should have realized with that question, that he was a serious competitor.

We were there an hour later, and so was he with a couple of his friends. This was only permissible because Brenda, the chaperone, was there to supervise. Thank the Lord for chaperones! We played cards for a couple hours. I was Rick's partner. He even yelled at me when I didn't play the *right* card. Italians have loud voices and definite opinions about things.

Then, after the game, he was walking me back to my room and we ended up talking, honest, until about 5:00 in the morning. I told him about Momma, about John, and the other stuff in between. He, being the wise, Bible college student, very matter of factly, told me to break up with John first thing in the morning.

I did and I've been *obeying* Rick ever since. Needless to say, John was not very happy. It was very painful for both of us. We had been through a lot together. But, when two people do not have the same call of God on their lives, the relationship becomes very unbalanced. Unbalanced = Unstable, and I knew I didn't need any more instability in my life.

Even through the tears, I knew I had done the right thing. I had a couple more days with Rick, but the answer to my fasting and prayer had come.

Milestone:

Obeying God's direction may not be easy, but you often have help in the process. (I had Brenda and Rick) God's word for your life does not originate with others, but can be confirmed through them. When choosing a mate for life, spiritual cohesiveness must be a major priority in the relationship. The first step may be painful, but the ones that follow hold untold facets of excitement.

On the bus ride home, John and I were NOT together. In fact, he had already hooked up with some other girl. Maybe just to hurt me, but it just confirmed God's plan to me.

When I got home, I remember telling Daddy and Regena, that I had met the man I was going to marry. I really didn't know if it would be Rick, but I knew now, that there were others out there for me. I just knew that I wanted it to be somebody like Rick Pasquale. I didn't know if I'd ever hear from Rick again. I figured he probably had a girl at every church the group had played at. But, I think his heart was smitten, too.

About a week later, I got a call from Rick. Well, actually, Daddy took the call. I was sleeping and not feeling well and Daddy told him I couldn't come to the phone and he'd have to call later. CAN YOU BELIEVE IT? The man of my dreams and prayers, and Daddy didn't wake me up. Daddy said, "If he really likes you, he'll call back." Maybe, but the waiting about killed me. However, when it's part of God's plan, the one formed *pre-delivery*, it's gonna happen. *"The steps of a righteous man/woman are ordered by the Lord".* Rick may not have known it, but he was destined to make that second call.

We saw each other a few times after that. His group would be ministering in one of our churches in Houston, and I would drive to see them. Sometimes, we would go out to dinner the night before the service.

One time, in particular, I guess Rick was starting to get serious about us and needed some "background" information on me. We were riding in the car and out of the clear blue, he said, "Are you a virgin?" My first thought was, how personal! But, I was, and I wanted him to know that. I also wanted him to know that I planned on staying that way until I got married. I didn't know it until later, but that answer is what made him want me.

Milestone:
This was one of those times, when I realized how important my talk with Daddy had been. Those times, when it had been hard to say No, but I did, had paid off. I was about to get the man of my dreams, because I had stayed true to myself and to God. Anything worth having is worth waiting for. Something new always makes a better gift than something used.

Now, what did I know about him? Rick is the oldest of five children in a very Italian family from Ohio. His grandparents were Catholic and then changed to Assembly of God, after his grandma got saved and had a real, personal encounter with Jesus Christ. Rick is a preacher's kid. His dad had always pastored small churches and served God wherever he could.

Consequently, with five children, they didn't have a lot of money. Their needs were always met, but as Rick and his brothers and sister would say, they ate a lot of fried bologna sandwiches. In fact, the only time Rick ever had a brand new bicycle, it got stolen the very next week. Everything was "hand-me-downs", goodwill, etc. The boys (there were four and one sister) always played sports. Actually, Linda, his sister, also played sports. She probably had to, to survive. I think this contributes to their drive to succeed.

Rick has always been very assertive in pursuing the will of God. He definitely knocks on doors, but he always waits for God to open it.

He was called into the ministry at summer youth camp. In fact, it was the scripture in Timothy, that said Preach the Word, that God used.

After running from the call for one year, by going to a secular college on a football scholarship, God knocked again, loudly. Rick had a hand injury and was not able to pursue professional sports. So, he went to Southwestern Assemblies of God College in Waxahachie, Texas.

Isn't it something? He's from Ohio. I'm from Texas. I went to college in Missouri. He went to college in Texas. We met in Colorado. That was God!

Milestone:
Never try to figure out how God is going to accomplish His will in your life. Don't put God in a box, or in a State. He is Omnipresent, and He can move the hearts of people in different places at different times for different events and ultimately blend it all together and create a masterpiece. Sometimes you have to go, before you know. Even Abraham had to follow God, without knowing where God was leading. But, it will always be confirmed through the Word of God.

CHAPTER 10

Before "I Do"

It seems that sometimes life goes so slow and other times you almost experience a lifetime in one short year. That's how it was for me after Daddy and Regena got married. Especially, after Tiffanie was born.

I had just finished my junior year of high school and was on my way to Stephen's College in Columbia, Missouri, as an advanced placement student. I was going to finish my senior year of high school and my freshman year of college at the same time.

During those college days, I lived with my dad's sister, Aunt Susie and her husband, Uncle Jerry. Daddy had said that if I was going to leave home a year early, I could not live on a college campus, but with family who could provide me with supervision and guidance. (This also provided Daddy with some assurance that his first born daughter would be watched over.) At the time, I didn't understand. I wanted to do the "dorm thing". But, looking back, I can see how *Father knew best*. I still got involved in a sorority, met friends on campus and had a great year.

I had already met Rick at the time and being at Aunt Susie's home did keep me somewhat sheltered, protected for the future.

Milestone:
Many things we don't understand in the present, are revealed as a part of God's plan later on. Again, the authority issue greatly affects our lives. Not only, if we obey the authority, but what is our attitude in the act of obedience? We must not stop living or put our lives on hold just because we can't see around the bend. In the car, we keep driving, by faith, trusting, that the road safely continues, always careful to follow the instruction signs along the way - Keep right. Caution! Stop. Proceed slowly. Construction completed, Continue on!

While I was at Stephen's, Rick would come to visit me. He was such a thrill in my life. He always had things under control and I felt safe with him. I went home for Christmas break and fully expected to receive a diamond from him. (We had been dating for one year.) However, I got a pair of diamond earrings, instead. I was still happy.

In March, I flew home from school for spring break. Instead of flying to Houston, I flew to Dallas. Rick was a youth pastor in Waco at the time. He was going to pick me up and then I would spend a few days with him, (staying in someone else's home, of course - again, Daddy still had a say in my life). Then, he would drive me to Houston.

Rick picked me up in his pastor's Continental. It was very classy, especially for a struggling, college student whose other choice would have been the green LeMans. We called it *the pickle*. Anyway, the Continental was a much better choice.

As he drove through downtown Dallas, on a very busy expressway, he suddenly pulled over on the shoulder of an overpass. Cars were whizzing past us and I was sure we would be killed in an accident. "What are you doing? What's wrong?", I asked.

Promptly, the native Buckeye from Ohio, began to give

me a lesson in Texas history. How all this city used to be a sandy, western town with saloons and gunfire. Before he could finish, I begged him to keep driving. Finally, he pulled back in to the lane of traffic, got off at the first exit, and pulled into an abandoned bar.

I was really getting nervous. My *Prince Charming* was trying to take me parking! However, Rick had a plan. He always does.

He leaned over and pulled a little box out of the glove compartment. He said, "I want you to remember every detail of this moment." (How could I forget; fear makes you remember!) He said, "Jennifer, I love you and I want to spend the rest of my life with you, making memories together. Will you marry me?" (Boy, was I relieved, not parking, after all.) Actually, I was ecstatic! Especially, when he opened the little box to reveal a beautiful diamond solitaire engagement ring from the same jewelry store we had browsed in together the past summer.

I was so in love with him. I said, "Yes, I love you". I think it was one of the few times in my life when I was at a loss for words.

We kissed, very sweetly and then Rick drove us to Waco. I didn't want to call Daddy with the news on the phone. This had to be in person. Whenever, you ask for something big, do it face to face.

Milestone:
If you don't settle for second best, allow God to be the keeper of the time clock, and TRUST HIM, He always gives you the very best. Also, when you need something from the Lord, meet Him face to Face. Or faith to Face. He said in Psalms 37, "Delight thyself also in the Lord; and He shall give thee the desires of thine heart. Commit thy way unto the Lord; trust also in Him; and He shall bring it to pass."

After Rick and I had spent a few days together, we drove to Houston. We walked in and had THE TALK with Daddy. (chapter 8, the milk glass incident). After that, I went back to school in Missouri and he went back to Waco.

We definitely had a long distance relationship. The phone company got rich off us, but the post office probably never knew our name. I have two letters from Rick. One, he sent shortly after we met that was very newsy and UNemotional, courteously signed, Love, Rick. The other one, he sent to me after we were engaged, just before the wedding. I think it said, I Love You, about 17 times. What a romantic.

The last quarter of school went by quickly. I don't remember a lot about events at school.

I remember Uncle Jerry taking me to a University of Missouri football game. That was fun. Rick played football, but I never got to see him, so I just imagined what it would feel like, if that was him out there on that field.

Aunt Susie taught me, through gentle reminders to keep the bathroom clean. I still do today; at least it's on the priority list. It was like a lot of people in my life were finishing the lessons that Mother never got to teach me. I am so glad that they got involved and were not afraid to get involved in my growing process. I may not have always been the best student, but some things you learn with practice.

Uncle Jerry also taught me how to balance my check book. Math was not my favorite subject, so I'm sure this took a lot of patience on his part. Especially, when you have to work in the negative. I still balance the checkbook for our household, now. Thankfully, not as much in the negative.

Milestone:

Sometimes, it's the little things that help us in practical ways. The checkbook, the house cleaning, the game. I was learning to appreciate the things that would make my house run more smoothly. Some things you learn now, but don't use until later.

In June, I came home to participate in my High School graduation ceremonies at Eisenhower High School. Once again, Regena worked to make it special, along with Daddy, of course.

Grandma and Papa Schaffer were there, Rick was there, some of Regena's family, and a chapter was closing.

It was just a few short weeks later, that Rick and I were married. I wouldn't recommend this kind of timing for my daughters, but when it's God's plan, it works. I hope I remember this. Sometimes, we think it's only good for us, but, God works in mysterious ways.

The summer of 1978 was much better than the summer of 1975. It was like Phase II was now beginning. I lost a lot in 1975, but God was definitely restoring all of us. I would have given anything if Mother had been there to share those special moments with me. I will be honest. I did struggle with how unfair it still seemed. A girl needs her mother. Daddy and Regena were both wonderful, but it's just not the same. I never said *Stepping Forward* was easy. Some things we never understand. I told someone I was making a list of questions to ask the Lord when I get to Heaven, and they replied, "It won't matter once you get there."

Milestone:

Even if the purpose of God's plan is not revealed along the way, there is good in every situation. But there is one condition: you get what you put in to it. Life is a process of investments and returns, deposits and withdrawals. When the account gets low, you have to take the time to build up the equity again. If you don't, you will move so swiftly along the road, that you miss the landmarks of beauty along the way. You might get there quicker than I do, but at whose expense? And with how much enjoyment? Remember, five steps forward and two steps back is still only three steps. However, as long as you are moving ahead, you're going in the right direction. Never give up!

There are wonderful surprises around those sharp corners.

CHAPTER 11

The Honeymoon Years

Considering the fact that Rick and I had only been together eleven or twelve times in the past year and a half, and considering the fact that he was a Yankee and I was a Texan, and considering the fact that he was from a big, Italian family, and I was from small, southern roots, we had a lot of getting to know each other in the first two years.

We had a three day honeymoon in Galveston, Texas, and then drove to Chickamauga, Georgia with all our worldly possessions, which happened to be one very small trailer attached to the back of our black and white 1975 Monte Carlo, (a present from my dad), to begin a new youth ministry at the Gospel Tabernacle Assembly of God.

Rev. Edwin Smith, and his wife, Wanda, (author of the song, Harvest Time), and their son, Eddie, became our boss/family. We lived with the Smiths for about three months, until the church could afford to purchase a mobile home for us. They parked it right on the church property. How convenient! It was nice to be able to make it to church in less than two minutes. However, it was a little inconvenient when someone came to the door, just minutes after you had stepped out of the shower. I didn't let anybody see me without make-up in those days. (A lot changes after three kids.)

We were in a very strict area and our pastor, Bro. Smith

made sure we always looked presentable. No shorts, not even for mowing grass in the hot, Georgia sun.

Milestone:
Even though restrictions can be restricting, we learned that it is very important to look your best. This body is the temple of the Holy Spirit, and we should not get lazy in taking care of it. Outward appearances draw people to you, if the appearance is good. Then, the inward appearance of your life draws them to Christ.

Another thing, I remember about Bro. and Sis. Smith, is that they loved people and people loved them. Bro. Smith spent more time out visiting than in the church office. He was teaching us that without people, there is no ministry.

Again, dependability is a necessary character trait for life, especially the minister's life. It's also important that, as spouses, we can depend on each other. Especially, in our situation, where my family was in Texas, and his family was in Ohio, we needed to be able to depend on each other.

We had a wonderful time of ministry in Chickamauga. In fact, many of our talents and skills were developed during that time. I went from not singing at all, to singing in the choir, then an ensemble, then a trio, then a duet, and finally, *A Solo*. Later, Rick and I even cut an album. Never, underestimate the power of God to increase your potential.

Milestone:
Never think, "I'm not good enough". Creator God makes no mistakes. It may sound corny, but He's more interested in our availability than our ability. "Not by might, nor by power, but by HIS spirit."

After Chickamauga, we moved to Ypsilanti, Michigan. (Rick had been in Waxahachie, Waco, Chickamauga, Ypsilanti. What's next, I thought. Kalamazoo? I didn't know this was a real place in Michigan. We never lived there, but we have ministered there. I was just praying for an address that I could spell.) Rick's parents had moved to Ypsilanti, after Rick's dad accepted the pastorate there.

Dad had called us and asked us to come for an interview. This was in the early eighties, when Associate Pastor, meant every department. We did accept the position and looked forward to being close to, at least some, of our family.

It was a wonderful four years! Rick and his dad learned to really appreciate the other's ministry and talents. Dad is a very hard worker and no one sits still under his ministry. We learned about every aspect of church work. We/Rick (we're one, so, it seemed like we) was the Youth Pastor, the Music Pastor, the Children's Pastor, the Bible Quiz Coordinator, the custodian, when necessary, and anything else that needed done. Those were not the days of *Specific* Ministry positions. We did all the jobs for one salary. But, God was faithful. I wouldn't trade those days for a million dollars. Although, I would have enjoyed a few extra dollars at the time. What a perspective we were gaining.

On top of all his church duties, Rick was the State Bible Quiz Coordinator, the State Youth Choir Director, sectional youth representative for all of Detroit, (over 80 churches), youth camp counselor and director and anything else he could get his hands on. The ministry was our life. But, we did it together. It didn't pull us apart, it pushed us closer.

We had people in our lives setting Godly examples, too. Rick's parents, of course, were not only great parents, great in-laws, but they were great teachers. They got us to Michigan, where God has used and blessed us for sixteen years. Gary and Jan Cullison, former Michigan Youth Directors, who allowed Rick the opportunity to minister in so many areas across the state and the globe. Rick is where he's at today, because Gary saw the potential in a young, youth pastor and his *availability,* and put him to work. *Now*, Rick is doing the same thing with other young, youth pastors. The cycle is always progressing.

Milestone:
If you're willing to do whatever, for the Lord, He will take the investment and triple the returns. Mentors are important, too. A mentor is someone who invests time, leadership, friendship, and personal commitment into another's life, not for the temporal rewards, but for the sake of eternity.

We took a youth group of 17, hard nosed kids and with the grace and love of God, turned it into a group of 75 or more of fired up kids for Christ. Several of those original 17, are in the ministry, today, either full-time or serving their churches as laity.

Milestone:
God is no respector of persons. Acts 10:34, Peter made this statement after he had betrayed Christ. He was realizing Christ's forgiveness in his own life. It doesn't matter who you are, who your parents are, what you did or what you do, the Blood covers it all.

Memory:
We had some great times those first five years of marriage and ministry, together. I remember lots of Sunday afternoons, spent at Mom and Dad's for homemade pasta and meatballs.

I had not become a connoisseur in the kitchen, yet.

I remember spending a few times in the emergency room with Mom, while Rick's two younger brothers, Jeff or Todd, were getting X-rays after injuring themselves in some athletic event. It always amazed me how calm Mom was. I guess after five children, you learn to just relax and roll with the tide.

I remember Sunday afternoon football games with the boys in the youth group. Rick was still a kid at heart. It was his opportunity to TACKLE some of the "tough" guys and get away with it. Investing time, emotionally fun, physically challenging.

I remember a few late, late phone calls from kids in the youth group, that were in trouble. Sleep might have been more relaxing, but the returns on the answered phone calls are still coming in.

One girl, Penny, had just overdosed and was in the emergency room. Her mother called us to come quickly. I think it was about 3:00 a.m. When we got there, I had to go in the room with Penny because her mother was so upset. Penny was in convulsions, wrenching and yelling, almost uncontrollable. I began to whisper the name of Jesus in her ear. I tried to hug her, reassure her, let her know that she was not alone, that she was loved. Pretty soon, she began to calm down.

Penny survived the experience and became a regular at our house, often past midnight. She needed counseling from someone outside of her family. We all do, sometimes. A neutral perspective. (Parents, don't take it personally, when your son or daughter wants outside instruction.)

Eventually, Penny got married. Today, she and her husband, are the Senior Pastors of a great church in Ohio. Who would have thought? Not Penny, maybe not us, (although, I think we did have high hopes for her,) but God knew. Remember Jeremiah?

Milestone:
He always has a plan, no matter how far away we get from it. II Corinthians 9:8, "And God is able to make all grace abound toward you; that ye, always having all sufficiency in all things, may abound to every good work."

While we were in Ypsilanti, our first daughter, Jacklyn Tennille Pasquale was born. Mother's namesake. Rick didn't even know Mother, but the minute Jacklyn was born, he said that should be her name. She's a lot like Mother, strong, independent, structured, intelligent and prissy. She's had a ponytail in her hair, since she was five months old.

Another wonderful thing I remember about the Ypsilanti days, was the closeness that developed between Rick's mom and I. She was there for me, when I was in labor. Rick was too, but we both needed Mom. She gave me the opportunity to say "Mom" again. It really felt nice. It still does. She was teaching me some more of those lessons that Mother wasn't able to finish. Like, making homemade spaghetti, a MUST in the Pasquale household.

I was learning just by watching her. She has always been so calm, so gentle, and so flexible. I have sometimes been a little "high strung", so it was good to be around her. I will probably do a whole chapter on her, too. She has been through more than one mother should have to endure, yet she remains faithful to God and her family. She's a saint!

Milestone:
Teaching life skills does not have to come out of a text book. In fact, some of the best training you can receive, can be done by watching someone else. Don't be afraid to ask questions. (Mom always has an ear to hear. Even if she doesn't have the answer, she's a terrific listener.) Parents need to

listen as much as talk. You teach self-esteem when you validate another's opinions just by listening.

The honeymoon years were about to come to a close. It had been several years since my tragedy of 1975. The marriage was strong, the ministry was prospering, and Rick, Jacklyn and I were moving into the next phase. Sometimes, you get ahead one step at a time, other times, it's one mile at a time. We were about to put many miles on the next stone.

CHAPTER 12

Traveling, Todd, Tragedy and Triumph

When Jacklyn was two years old, we left Ypsilanti Assembly of God to go on the Evangelistic field. Rick remembered how much fun it had been to travel in the group from college and he wanted to do it again, before we had kids in school.

We kept our home in Ypsilanti, bought a nice custom van, and started booking services. This was another one of those times when we would have one of those discussions with Daddy on following God's will, even though, you're not exactly sure what's around the corner. Daddy was concerned with finances for us. We would no longer have a guaranteed income. Would we be able to make the house payment? The van payment? Insurances?

A daddy never stops watching out for his children. It was, however, during this time, that Daddy really began to appreciate the essence of Rick. He saw that Rick got out there and got those services, (of course, it was the Lord providing them, but Rick was knocking), his ministry was prospering and people were getting saved, healed, and filled with the Holy Spirit under God's anointing on Rick's life. Not only, was Daddy trusting God with me, but he was realizing that he could trust Rick with me. Okay, so it took five years. Daddies don't let go. (Neither does Father God).

Milestone:
Proverbs 16:9, "A man's heart deviseth his way: but the Lord directeth his steps."

The evangelistic field was ripe and we were having fun, except for one small problem. MORNING SICKNESS! Can you believe I got pregnant two weeks after we left Ypsilanti? I do wonder about the Lord's timing. Actually, it was not just morning sickness, it was all day sickness. I was in the hospital twice, because of dehydration and losing weight. Finally, after five months of pregnancy, I was getting better. I could keep food down and the baby was growing. Suddenly, there was another sharp turn in the road.

We were in Houston, for services, when we got a call from Rick's brother, Michael. (We both have a brother, Michael and they both have a daughter, Rachel - interesting tidbit) Michael was calling from Kansas City.

Todd had just gotten out of the Air Force and was in K.C. visiting Michael. They had gone swimming at a friend's pool. Todd had done a one and a half somersault off the dive, without checking the depth of the pool. The pool was only six feet deep. (It should have never had a diving board installed.) Todd, extremely muscle bound, from working out in the military, hit the water at full force, crashed head first into the bottom of the pool, and came up in a dead man's float. Mike thought Todd was fooling around, showing him something he had learned in the Air Force. After several seconds, it looked as if Todd was dead. He would have been if Mike had not jumped in.

Todd was 6 ft., about 175 pounds of muscle. Mike was 5

ft. 7 in., about 145 pounds of skin and bones. This time, the FATHER was supervising the pool. With truly, supernatural strength, Mike managed to get Todd over to the side and up, out of the pool. He ran to call 911. (Unfortunately, this swimming experience did not turn out like mine.)

Todd had broken his neck. He was paralyzed from the neck down and on life support when we got to the hospital about twenty hours later. They had screwed pins in his temples, had him strapped to a straight board and he was turned with his face pointing towards the floor. Nothing underneath him.

We had just come from an outstanding revival. Rick had seen God heal a woman's back and lengthen her leg, right while he was praying for her.

He walked into that intensive care room, full of faith! I watched Rick as he got down on his hands and knees to crawl under that bed. He laid down on that cold, gray, hospital floor, on his back, and looked up, right into Todd's eyes. I watched as they both began to cry, Todd's tears dropping straight down on Rick's face and running off his cheeks, splashing on the floor. Rick was praying for Todd, interceding, pleading with God to intervene, immediately, and fully expecting all of the feeling to come back into Todd's body as he prayed.

Milestone Remembered:
Faith to Face. This was the biggest crisis the Pasquales had faced, and now we had to face God with our faith in His ability to take control of the situation.

I felt like I was reliving those moments of my own in an intensive care room, in 1975. My empathy for their grief was almost unbearable. Even when you understand someone else's pain, only God can heal the hurt. We had to put all of us in God's hands and we were all holding on tight.

My pregnant body was not handling this well, either. I would get nauseous and have to run to the nearest bathroom.

All of Rick's immediate family was there. We left Jacklyn with Rick's sister-in-law, Kim. She was staying home with her kids and calling family to pray and answering phone calls for the family.

I don't remember how long Todd was in the hospital in Kansas City. I think it was about three months before he could be moved. It was life and death for many days. Finally, he was transferred to the University of Michigan Hospital in Ann Arbor, Michigan. There, he stayed for several more months, learning to swallow again, learning how to take care of his body, going through rehabilitation therapy.

According to doctors, and the injury, Todd will never walk again. He regained some strength in his left shoulder and can operate an electric wheel chair with his wrist. All bodily functions are taken care of by someone else. His blood pressure has to be constantly monitored. Someone has to feed him, bathe him, brush his teeth, etc.

The strong, good looking, muscle bound Air Force recruit is now going through some changes of his own. Changes that will last a lifetime. Emotional changes as well as physical changes.

He lost his girlfriend, Joni. At least, she was honest enough to say from the start, that she just couldn't handle it. She has stayed his friend for many years. That was just the first of a series of tragedies for Todd.

He later married and after two and a half years, his wife left him.

He later had a heart attack and even told Mom NOT to call 911. He has had to make a constant choice for life in the last ten years.

Were we discouraged because God did not raise Todd up?

Was our faith destroyed? Discouraged, yes, destroyed, NO!

Milestone:

God is sovereign! He is in control! He won't give us more than we are able to bear! He will push us to the limit, or at least, allow us to be pushed. He is as close as the mention of His name. I trust God, not because of what He does, but because of who He is. Remember, in order to look forward, we have to look back, at the cross. We have to look at Christ's sufferings. Christ cried out to His Father, "Why hast thou forsaken me?" He knows our pain, he feels our sorrow, he suffered our afflictions. I Corinthians 15:57, "But thanks be to God, which giveth us the victory through our Lord Jesus Christ." I Corinthians 13:7, "Love beareth all things, believeth all things, hopeth all things, endureth all things." I John 4:8, "God is love." Seek God in the midst of EVERY situation, good and bad. Jeremiah 29:11-13, "For I know the thoughts that I think toward you, saith the Lord, thoughts of peace, and not of evil, to give you an expected end. Then shall ye call upon me, and ye shall go and pray unto me, and I will hearken unto you. And ye shall seek me, and find me, when ye shall search for me with all your heart." No matter what, I must seek God. I can not make it through life's difficulties without Him and I do not want to experience life's goodness apart from Him.

The year Todd had his diving accident was very tragic. However, it ended in triumph. On December 13, 1984, Jessica Danielle Pasquale was born and life continued. Todd's life continued, too. Even though he would not rock Jessica on his lap, like he had done for Jacklyn, and he would not paint the garage with graffiti again, (little brothers are pesky at times, actually, my brother, Michael helped Todd with the graffiti), he would not wrestle his brothers anymore, (he always beat them), and he would not run physically anymore, he was not out of the game. He has been running one of the best games of his life for the last ten years. He survived the divorce, bought property, bought a grocery store, is involved with Eastern Michigan University's athletic department, helps coach basketball camp in the summer and brings extreme joy and laughter to all who know him, especially my three daughters, who think he is the coolest.

Milestone:
Never give up in the face of adversity. Sometimes, even death seems easier. "But to live is Christ and to die is gain" Until God calls each of us home, to live for Him is to live a life, abundant and full.

CHAPTER 13

"Saint" Joan

One thing for sure, the life of Joan Pasquale has never been boring. If it gets any fuller, someone else may have to take over.

My mother-in-law has got to be on the Saint roster in Heaven. She has five children, four boys and one girl. She has a husband who can fix anything, including dinner, but leaves a "tornado aftermath" for her to clean up. She could write an entire book on the life and times of being Rick, Mike, Linda, Jeff, and Todd's mother. She could write a book on being married to R.J. Pasquale. Instead, I would like to try to highlight some of the momentous events in this chapter.

When we look back at Joan's life, we can't help but step forward, because we see how far we have all come.

I guess the first major hurdle, was son, Michael. Somewhere, along the way, Mike got away from God. He married Kim, had three great kids, lived in Kansas City, Missouri, and had his own auto body shop. But, it wasn't enough. Mike needed a thrill and he found it in Cocaine. But, the Cocaine took the thrill out of Mike's life. He nearly lost his family, his house, he did lose his business, and almost his own life.

The hours that Joan spent praying and crying for her son. For over fifteen years, she prayed. She loved him no matter what he did. She kept in touch with him and his family. Finally, after a couple unsuccessful attempts to clean up his life, Mike gave himself completely to the Lord. It was awesome to see the joy on Mom's face, the tears in her eyes, and the peace in her mind. God came through!

Milestone:
Never give up! "The effectual, fervent prayers of a righteous man, availeth much." Even when they are prayed for the unrighteous. Keep loving your children, no matter what they do. Even if they disappoint you, you are their parent. Just like our relationship with Father God. Even when we disappoint Him, He's still the one who gave us life. We are linked for eternity.

Next, I guess you could say, it was Todd. His tragedy changed her life as well as his. Before Todd had his accident, Mom and Dad had just begun enjoying a new phase in their life. All the children were grown and gone and they were alone with each other. I could tell she was really enjoying her independence. She would help me with my kids, work at church, organize ladies' events, and was the State Missionettes Coordinator. Life was full and Joan was finally getting to do something for herself. Not that she had ever complained or begrudged being a stay-at-home mom. I knew she loved her children; she did everything for them. (Rick probably never made a bed in his life. He still leaves that blessing for me.) But, now, it was her turn and she was enjoying this phase too.

Suddenly, I'm sure it was as if her car had careened off a ravine and was forever tumbling into a dark crevasse, with no rescue personnel in sight. She was there for Todd, though. She and Dad got to Kansas City as fast as they could and I doubt if she ever left the hospital those first few days.

After Todd was brought home, and rehabilitated at the

U. of M. hospital, he came back home to live. Mom could no longer go anywhere, not even for a few minutes, without making sure there would be someone there to take care of Todd. She always fed Todd before she fed herself, consequently, she has had thousands of cold dinners in the last twelve years.

Just about the time she thought her work was done, and would sit down to take a short break, Todd would call. He would need to be repositioned or have his nose scratched. Mom, always without complaint, would get up and take care of him.

She had to dress him again. She probably hadn't done that for fifteen years, and it was a lot more difficult with his six foot frame and limp body. She has physically lifted him in and out of the wheel chair and the bed too many times to count. She chauffeurs him wherever he needs to go.

When Todd bought the grocery store, Mom quit her job at the florist (she loves to work with flowers), and helped Todd manage the store. She had given Todd life, and she knew it was the gift that keeps on giving.

When he was married, she had a little break, but Todd still needed her then, because his wife just couldn't take care of him like Mom.

When Todd got divorced, Mom rearranged her family room once again, to become Todd's bedroom, because it was accessible to the wheel chair. She even recently got robbed while working at the grocery store, but still, she keeps on giving.

Milestone:
The stamina required to be a parent for life, make that a good parent for life, has to be supernaturally given. If you're trying to make it without Divine Intervention, you're not using all the blocks available. The Word of God gives instructions

to the parents, It gives comfort to the parent who feels the despair of the situation, It gives hope to the hopeless, It gives strength to the weary, It is the blueprint for life. The ultimate book on "Blended Families". Why wouldn't you use it? At least, read it. Through everything, I have never seen Mom lose her faith. I have never heard her blame God. I'm sure she's had her private talks with Him, but she continues to trust Him.

Next, there was Jeff. He was number four in the birth order. According to his brothers and sister, slightly spoiled. But, Jeff was a good kid. He graduated from high school, and went on to North Central Bible College for three years. Then, Todd had his accident. (Tragedies tend to have a ripple effect).

Jeff had decided to go into the Army to be a military chaplain. The first discouragement for him, was when his superior told him to not use the name of Jesus, but rather, the Higher Power, thereby relating to all religions. Jeff knew Jesus is the Way and he wanted to share the gospel with men in need of direction.

Secondly, Jeff had a very hard time accepting Todd's accident. How could God, a loving, merciful Father, allow this to happen? This was a natural question. But, one that defies answers. Suddenly, Jeff had no direction. He was disillusioned with life. He just took off. No one knew where he was. He was missing for almost three months. Joan was incapacitated with worry. Was he dead? Had someone hurt him?

Finally, Rick's dad found Jeff in Missouri, working door to door as a salesman. He convinced him to come home. It was like the Prodigal son. Mom prepared his dinners, made his bed, washed his clothes and endured painful silences from Jeff. He was just unable to explain his feelings or his actions.

Today, Jeff still lives at home. He helps with Todd, helps at the store, and enters into the family as much as he chooses. And, Mom accepts him. We all do. He's family and part of God's creation, whether he recognizes it or not. Mom loves him, too. We all do.

Milestone:
Parents must accept their children even when they don't do what we would have expected for them. Forgiveness is an action, not a conversation. Someone once said you should raise a child with the four L's: Love, listening, laughter, and loyalty. Mom had practiced all of these with Jeff and the others, but with Jeff, especially loyalty.

I do not wish to betray any family confidences, but it is a story with tremendous love and perhaps, if shared, will cause other families to fight less, forgive more, and love always. The Italians are known for loyalty. Obviously, according to the depiction of the Mafia, you don't mess with the family. The Pasquales are not the Mafia, but they are loyal to each other. If you're loyal to your earthly family, you'll learn to be loyal to God. To be true to Him, no matter what tempts you. LOYALTY!

Next, there's Linda. The only girl, Mother's little helper. Mom and Linda had a really great relationship. They shared a common interests in crafts, cooking, boys, (Linda has two) and a love and understanding for the Pasquale men.

But, something happened that put a great chasm of silence between them. It was almost a year or more, before their relationship was mended. The pain that Mom felt, to lose a daughter, emotionally, though, not physically. But, Joan did not give up. She kept trying. She wrote Linda. She invited her to dinner. And she tried to understand Linda's perspective. Thank the Lord, they are close again. (I always hurt for those Mother/daughter relationships that are not enjoying time together, because I know how special this relationship is, and how quickly, you can lose it.)

Milestone:

Mother/daughter relationships take a lot of work. Women can be very emotional and unpredictable at times. I've been a daughter, now I'm a mother to daughters, and I've watched numerous other mother/daughter relationships. There has to be give and take on both sides of the relationship. We must try to put ourselves in each other's shoes, from time to time. It will help the understanding process, immensely. Daughters need independence from their mothers. Mothers want to hold their daughters, (even their sons), forever. Moms need to give their daughters space once in a while and daughters need to give more hugs.

The "Momma bird" prepares a nest for her babies, before they come. She stays in the nest while they are developing. She feeds them, sings to them, teaches them to fly, to soar. Then, she lets them go. The "baby bird" never returns to the "mom's" nest. In fact, the baby bird goes and begins another cycle of life. We could take a lesson from these little creatures of "Father" God. Luke chapter 12 reminds us, that not one sparrow is overlooked by God. He knows when they drop from the nest. As "Momma birds", we must begin to trust "Father" God to watch over our little "sparrows" for us, after they "drop from our nests". No need to worry, God is in control!

Finally, regarding *Saint Joan*, she has been a faithful and loving helpmate for R.J. Pasquale for almost forty years. She's worked with him in small churches, big churches, church building programs, and home building projects. She's moved her *nest* several times to follow God's direction for R. J.'s ministry. Even now, she's at home alone, many months out of the year.

Dad is now a Missionary Evangelist with the Assemblies of God. He has traveled to India, the Philippines, Africa, Malaysia, Argentina, and many other places at home and abroad. Even though, Joan does not usually go with him, she is part of every soul that makes heaven, because of Dad's ministry. She loves God and therefore, it just comes naturally to her, to love people.

Milestone:

As I have observed Joan Pasquale, over the last eighteen years, I have learned so much. I have enjoyed her company, appreciated her support, and cherished the memories in the making. She has shown me that right priorities, help keep your life in perspective. If your priorities are straight, you just take circumstances, one stone at a time. Sometimes, it might feel like you're being "stoned", other times, you might wish you were "stoned", and other times, it will seem as though all the stones are creating a great masterpiece of artwork. It's called the tapestry of life. There are many textures, many fabrics and colors, many seemingly insignificant threads, and other beautifully ornate threads interwoven to make the magnificent cording that frames the piece. There are many lives interwoven in ours that make us God's masterpiece. If one thread begins to unravel, you could lose the whole fabric. That's why every thread is important, though, not always seen or recognized by those that gaze upon the masterpiece. These are few of those unseen threads in Joan's life that have been woven together to create a masterpiece of love and gentleness. I love you, Mom!

CHAPTER 14

Ministry Memories

We have been very blessed in our life. Every one of our ministry opportunities have been totally awesome! We have had the privilege of serving some of the finest Senior Pastors in the nation. Each one has taught us, loved us, and stretched us to do more for God.

Chronologically, they are as follows:

Waco, Texas - Pastor Paul Palser

Rick served Pastor Palser as Youth Pastor for about a year. We were not married yet, however, Rick learned things in Waco, that do affect us both. For example, GOLF. It really was more than just golf. For every golf game, that Rick and Pastor Palser had together, they were building a friendship. Pastor Palser was truly Rick's mentor. And, because of golf in our lives today, I can shop without feeling guilty. After all, we all need recreation.

Milestone:
It is important to build relationships with the people you work with. "No man is an island". It's a lot more fun to serve those

who appreciate us in a variety of ways. It is also a lot easier to lead those whom you have invested personal time with. No, this is not risky! In our society today, we must have those in our lives to whom we can be accountable. It will keep us pure, in thought, motive, action, and deed.

Chickamauga, Georgia - Pastor Edwin Smith

This was our first ministry together. Rick was the Associate Pastor, mainly in charge of youth. As I have already recorded, we lived on the church property. I remember many practical jokes we used to play on each other.

One time, my brother, Michael was staying with us. Rick and the music pastor left the trailer, and went over to the church to check on something. The next thing, Michael and I knew, Terry, the music pastor, came busting through the back door! "Somebody's in the church! I think they got Rick!", he said. I was frantic and Michael hid behind the couch. Just as I was about to call Pastor Smith, receiver in hand, Rick nonchalantly walks through the door. He and Terry just busted out laughing. Michael had gotten his bebe gun and was ready to shoot. I guess we all laughed about it later, but it was pretty scary.

I remember building a ten foot snowman, the only time it probably ever snowed in Chickamauga. Rick had me on his shoulders, to put the hat on the snowman. We took a picture. It was fun!

I remember going to football games to watch kids in our youth group. I remember "Pentecostal Handshakes". (That's when someone shakes your hand and leaves a twenty dollar bill in your hand, or more, after the shake.) It was God's way of providing for us when we had just scrapped the last of the peanut butter jar, or eaten the last pot pie.

I remember being lonely. One time I sat on Rick's lap in

our little single wide mobile home on our "hand-me-down" furniture, and we both cried. (We had just gotten married and moved hundreds of miles away from all family and friends.)

I remember being "adopted" by families in the church, who would invite us out to eat, and THEY PAID!

It was a time of learning, about each other as well as about ministry together.

Milestone:

In the ministry, it is imperative that your spouse becomes your best friend. Friendships are built upon giving. I had to learn to give support, not instruction. (Like I really knew more than Rick. He was the preacher's kid, I was the engineer's kid. I do have good ideas though. I just had to learn how and when to express them.) Rick had to learn to accept me and to nurture my gifts and talents. There's a fine line between leading and dragging. Rick was learning to lead. I developed the ability to sing. Talents aren't always inherited. Sometimes they are learned, always with practice.

Ypsilanti, Michigan - Pastor R.J. Pasquale

The four years Rick served in Ypsilanti as Associate Pastor were incredible family building times. Our ministry in Michigan was also established during these years. We did everything. The Singing Christmas Tree, children's church, Bible Quiz (our team made it to Nationals, then won Nationals the year after we left), Youth ministry, church secretary (that was my job), parenting began with the birth of Jacklyn (we had the cutest Raggedy Ann and Andy baby shower), and lots more I don't remember.

The best thing about Ypsilanti, was being with Rick's family. They learned to appreciate us both as adults and fellow laborers in the Harvest. We learned to appreciate their wisdom, their drive to get the job done, their unconditional love (I'm sure we made some mistakes, but they were always forgiven).

Milestone:

You are never too old to take instruction from your father. (Especially, when he's your boss.)

Family loyalty is one of the most precious gifts you can give to your children. (Mom and Dad were always there, supporting our ministry efforts. That meant so much.)

Family dinners make the best opportunity for family milestones. Everyone sitting down to eat, at the same time, at the same table, is an art that must not be forgotten. (This family has the BEST spaghetti in the world!)

The Evangelistic Field - Rick's his own boss

We traveled for almost two years. We made our famous (?) cassette album. Jessica was born during this time. We did a lot of singing and preaching. (That must be why Jacklyn and Jessica are always wanting their chance to be on stage. We were doing it as adults, they were practicing as children.) What children see and live with, affects them greatly. It is a big responsibility to provide a wholesome environment. It is not an impossibility, even in today's society. We were together almost twenty four hours a day, seven days a week, fifty two weeks a year. It was a blast! Well, the packing and unpacking wasn't so fun, but the sight-seeing was terrific.

Milestone:
If you're willing to let God open some unexpected doors, you will experience some unexpected joys. Flexibility is the key to a happy and UNfrustrated life. You can call it adventure or adversity. It's up to your attitude. This was an adventure. Also, God blesses those who give. This was a time of tremendous blessing.

St. Clair Shores, Michigan - Pastor Paul Sundell

Rick was the Senior Associate Pastor, in charge of Youth ministry. This was the church of Rick's culinary dreams. Every church social had pasta, because the congregation was predominately Italian. Rick was in "pasta heaven". Our ministry was so exciting here. We started with about thirty five to fifty youth. Almost four years later, in our last youth service there, we had almost three hundred.

I remember some awesome winter retreats, where the Spirit of God came and transformed all of our lives.

I remember some incredible kids, who got transformed by the power of God and then went and transformed their high schools. One girl brought over thirty kids to youth group in one year. She's in the ministry today. She also "preached" at her public high school graduation ceremony.

I remember Frank Mazzie and his wife, Kay. He was the church's Business Administrator and he is Italian. They are still in our life today. Frank taught Rick the importance of giving to the Lord. Not only, in dollars, but in actions. "God deserves our best effort", Frank would say. Frank also made Rick accountable. To this day, Rick's financial paper work is done with the utmost integrity and detail. It has become one of his strengths.

Pastor Sundell was a man of the Word. He taught Rick, by example, to have good study habits. Everyone at St. Clair

Shores gave us the joy of serving and ministering.

Milestone:
There is learning to be done in every situation. If I'm not learning, I'm probably not growing. The blessings of God come in a variety of packages, through a variety of people. Never turn away the "little" packages, sometimes they contain the best surprises. Never minimize the giftings in other people. Strong leaders help others maximize their talents.

Grand Rapids, Michigan - Rick Pasquale, Senior Pastor

This has got to be one of the highlights of our life and ministry. Our first Senior Pastor position, and it could not have been better.

The church grew from 75 to 250 in three years. Our last Easter there, we had 401 in attendance. We went to two Sunday morning services. We went through a building program while there, enlarging the foyer, adding Sunday School classrooms, fellowship hall, bathrooms, and a new executive office wing. It was so exciting!

In the four years we were there, we lived in four places. When we first moved there, we lived in an apartment, while we were having a house built. It was a two bedroom, two bath apartment. It was adequate, but we were a little tight on closet space. (Four girls!) Then, we moved to our first NEW home. It was so pretty. We had plenty of space to entertain, inside as well as outside. We had lived in this house about a year, when we started the building program at church. Rick and I had talked about giving, *substantially*, to help in this endeavor.

One Sunday, Rick decided, while I was downstairs in the nursery, to announce to the congregation, that we were going to sell our home, so we would have $5,000 to give to the building fund. I remember Jacklyn, running into the nursery, crying, "Momma, Daddy said we're moving!" I was trying to act like I was totally in control, for the sake of other ladies in the nursery, who were looking at me, like, "What in the world?" "We're not moving, honey.", I responded. About that time, another lady came down to the nursery. "Oh yes, you are, according to Pastor." Boy, was I in a jam. I needed to console Jacklyn. I did not want people to think that the Pastor and I had not communicated to each other. (Although, that was exactly the situation.) I wanted to be consoled myself, as I could not imagine selling my house. Where were we going to live?

Well, we did sell. We did give $5,000.00 to the church. We moved into another two bedroom apartment, much smaller, ONE bathroom. (Four girls!) "The things you do for love." Rick later apologized to me and the girls, for not talking through this decision in private, first. Like I said, we are always learning. There were so many milestones happening in our lives during this time.

Milestone:
Talk to your wife, before you take away her "nest"! Let your husband lead and follow with joy! If a mistake gets made, he'll be responsible for it. Include the ENTIRE family in the decisions that affect them.

During this time, of moving and building, we knew God was in control. The church was exploding. We had over 1,500 kids at an Easter Egg Hunt in the city park. Families were being drawn to our church through many ways, including the yellow pages. Two sisters came this way. They gave their hearts to God, and before we knew it, fifty of their family and friends had done the same and started coming to our church. How humbling to be used by God in such an awesome way. Yes, we made a sacrifice of convenience, by selling our home. But, God's word is TRUE! "Give and it shall be given." We could not contain the blessings of God, physically, financially, and spiritually.

After six months in the tiny apartment, our beautiful dream home across the street from the lake, was completed. This was a very fun and busy time. We had done all of the general contracting and oversight of this 3500 square foot home. It really didn't start out to be so big, but God blessed us in every area, making the dollar go a lot further than we had expected.

A lot of people have told me that when they built a house, it almost ruined their marriage. I guess for us, it was definitely the right time and God was definitely in control. It was really one of the highlights in our marriage. We had so much fun doing this project. Yes, there were some very stressful moments and a lot of long hours. The church was growing and there was some expansion construction going on at the church at the same time. (I felt like I was doing the "doggie paddle" again, but His Grace was sufficient. I'm also sure that the memories and milestones we had built together in previous years, were the strong foundation keeping this "house" together.)

When we finally did move in, we had some wonderful church fellowships at the house and felt abundantly blessed. It was truly a very memorable time in our lives and ministry. As I am remembering, I am constantly aware that my life has been full of extremes - extreme highs and extreme lows. I don't think I have ever had a truly "boring" month, since the day I said, "I Do". The days in Grand Rapids were exceptionally intense!

Assemblies of God, Michigan District
- Rick Pasquale, District Youth Director-

Rick has had many dreams and plans in his life, but there was one very special one. When Rick was a teenager, the D-CAP (District Christ's Ambassador's President) in Ohio, was very instrumental in Rick's life. Ray Rachels planned some awesome summer youth camps, where God called Rick in to the ministry. Rick had wanted to grow up and be a D-CAP like Ray Rachels ever since I met him.

We had moved in to our house in Grand Rapids on Saturday, and Rick left to go to a State Ministers' Conference on Monday. I stayed home to handle some last minute plumbing completions at the new house and went to join Rick on Tuesday. I had only unpacked the necessary bedding and kitchen boxes and left the rest to do when I got home. After all, I'd be in this house for many years. (I forgot to expect the unexpected.)

When I got to the hotel where the conference was being held, I saw a few of our friends as I came in the lobby. "Have you seen Rick!", they were asking me. "Have you heard?", someone said. "Heard what?" I replied. Steve Bach, the current D-Cap of the Michigan Assemblies of God, had just resigned. Some of our friends knew of Rick's dream and thought he might be in line for this position. I blocked out every thought like that. We just built our dream home. We were pastoring the dream church and God was moving incredibly. This was just not the time for this.

When I got to our room on the fifth floor, I let myself in with the key I had picked up at the front desk. I found Rick. He was sick in the bathroom. "What's the matter?" I asked, my heart racing. Rick told me of Steve's resignation and that the District Superintendent, Bro. Leach, had told Rick he wanted to talk to him.

I didn't even hesitate. "No! Absolutely not!" I didn't

need to pray about this, it was obvious. It just wasn't God's timing. How could it be?

Milestone:
We see things from an earthly perspective with the calendar in mind. God directs our lives from His supernatural vantage point and He has eternity in view.

Well, to make a long story short; after three months of prayer, fasting, interviews, board meetings, and phone calls to parents, Rick made the decision. He accepted the position. I say Rick made the decision. Every time we have ever made a change in our lives, we have agreed together. When I know the "head of our household" is seeking God's will and not his own and he has prayed and fasted and sought Godly counsel, I have to follow that. I have complete trust in someone who puts their complete trust in God. God does not make mistakes!

It has been almost five years now and it has been incredible. The position is now called the District Youth Director. It is a position with a variety of ministry opportunities and it has been the most incredible ride so far.

Nothing is easy. It wasn't easy to leave that house, that church, our friends and our dreams for that community. But, it's God's church, God's people and God's plans are the best. The church in Grand Rapids is prospering and our family has prospered in this calling. Watching God give Rick his "teenage dream" has been so wonderful. It has kept us young and in touch with today's generation.

I guess the main thing I have learned from all of our ministry changes, is that God never changes! He is the constant in my life. His grace sustains, His peace comforts, His joy delights, His love endures.

Milestone:
When your life is changing, and you don't know what direction to go, Look up! When you don't want to look ahead and you can't bear to look back, Look up! In other words, TRUST GOD! Ask Him to guide you and then trust and follow His leading. You won't always see the total picture, but just take it one frame at a time, one step at a time.

CHAPTER 15

Four Months in Bed! My Miracle in Progress

I know, you're probably thinking, "What can be better than cancer cured?" Being raised from the dead!

It all started in November, 1992. Rick and I and the girls had gone to a convention at the Opryland Hotel in Nashville, Tennessee. The night before we were scheduled to leave, Rick received word that his uncle had died in New York. Rick left right away, leaving me and the girls to check out and drive the car back home to Michigan.

The next morning, when it was time to check out, I got a little bit turned around in that big hotel facility. I had high heels on, was carrying a big suitcase in one hand and carrying Ericka on the other side, propping her up on my hip. Jacklyn and Jessica were dragging the rest of the suitcases behind. Why I didn't get a Bellman, I'll never know. Believe me, it would have been worth the tip. Anyway, I probably ended up walking a mile or so around that place trying to find the correct check out lobby and then going to another lobby where Valet was stationed, to retrieve the car. Needless to say, I probably got a few discs out of alignment in my back.

When we got back to my Grandma's house where we were going to stay for a bit, I was tired and sore, but didn't think much of it. Later, I bent over to brush out my hair. I had very long hair, past my shoulders, at the time. I flung my hair back and lifted up quickly and when I did, I heard something snap. I felt immediate pain in my neck and almost blacked out. I could feel the pain running down my neck and into my arm and right down to my fingertips. I went ahead and finished getting ready and loaded the girls in the car. Jacklyn had to sit behind me and literally hold my shoulders steady, because every time I moved the car forward or stopped to brake, the slightest movement would send excruciating pain through my neck and I would feel like I would pass out.

I don't know how, but I drove all the way home to Michigan in that condition. After we got home, a few days went by and I'm not really sure if the pain subsided or if I just got used to it. This was just a few months after Rick had resigned as Pastor at our church in Grand Rapids, and he had assumed the role of District Youth Director for the Assemblies of God in Michigan. Therefore, he was doing a lot of traveling. The district office was in Dearborn and we still owned our home in Grand Rapids.

Rick was commuting back and forth, about a three hour drive. He would go to Dearborn on Monday and come home on Thursday night. If he had a service scheduled on the east side of the state, sometimes he would just stay there. So, I was without him quite a bit. I was trying to be a good mother, faithful wife, and feeling terrible pain every day. Sometimes I would get the two older girls off to school, set Ericka in front of the TV, take three Extra Strength Tylenols, and collapse on the couch.

Finally, in late January of 1993, we moved over to the east side of the state. I finally went to see a doctor. The new job provided great insurance. However, because I had not been seen by any doctors in that system yet, the process for treatment was very slow!

After several visits, months of pain, physical therapy, and lots of crying, they sent me to a specialist. They had been giving me muscle relaxers, pain pills, and steroids to shrink swelling, but nothing was working and the situation was getting worse daily.

Rick had been gone so much and I would be at home with the girls, many times asleep from the medicine. I tried to explain to the doctor that this just wasn't working. I needed an answer. What was wrong with my neck? Why was I in so much pain? And, why hadn't it gotten better in time, like the doctor had suggested it would? At first, they thought I had just pulled a muscle, then sprained a ligament, then, they just didn't know. Oh boy, was I getting frustrated!!

I had talked to God. I had *begged* Him to take this condition away. I just wasn't getting any answers anywhere. The more time I spent in bed, the more it hurt. The longer it hurt, the worse the condition seemed to be getting.

Finally, I began to get numb in my left arm. I could no longer hold things in my left hand. I dropped a scalding cup of hot water, because of my loss of muscle control. I was becoming paralyzed in my left arm!

Finally, the specialist ordered an MRI scan of the neck and shoulder area. A few days later, he called Rick and I to come in to his office. He showed us the pictures taken from the MRI. My disc between the fifth and sixth vertebrae had ruptured. Fragments were pressing in on my spinal cord, causing the paralysis in my left arm. I had two options. I could live with the pain and condition as it was, which might get worse. Or, I could have surgery, removing the disc and replacing the empty space with a bone from my hip; there would be some risks to the surgery, as well.

I was in so much pain, and terribly afraid of the paralysis

spreading. We knew very well, from Rick's brother, Todd, that this was no minor problem. I had been almost flat on my back in bed for four weeks and I was ready to be well.

We decided on the surgery. The doctor said he had done over one thousand surgeries with about a 99% success rate. I would actually be having two surgeries at once. The one to remove the ruptured disc and one to remove a pencil size piece of bone from my hip to be inserted in my neck between the discs.

Rick asked the doctor if I would need any blood. Rick wanted to donate it ahead of time, if so. The doctor said, "No, she'll probably only lose about an ounce of blood. Unless I cut an artery, then she would bleed to death and you couldn't give her enough blood." That was encouraging? He told us he had to tell us of the risks, due to malpractice situations. He was just trying to give us possible scenarios, but we had nothing to worry about. This surgery has been done many times and this had never happened.

I called my daddy. "I need you.", I told him. I wanted him to come and stay with the girls while I was in the hospital and then to stay with me when I came home. I would be in bed for a while. He said he would come. My daddy has always been there for me. I know I'm blessed. It was also going to be Ericka's birthday. We arranged for Rick's secretary to take Ericka to her birthday party at Chuck E. Cheese, back in Grand Rapids. Since we had just moved, Ericka really hadn't made any new friends here yet. Ericka says that was the worst day of her life, "When Momma missed my birthday." She did have a great party though.

The time arrived for surgery. I went in to the hospital a few days early, because I had to have a Milogram prior to surgery. This would enable the doctor to see in even more detail, how fragmented the disc was. I was not allowed to eat for twelve hours prior. The Milogram was very painful and I was getting a Migraine headache from not eating. Then, I had to wait another twenty four hours for the surgery.

I was wheeled into the operating room on Saturday afternoon. As the doctor and nurses were prepping me, I asked if I could pray before they put me to sleep. They obliged and I prayed. I can't imagine what might have happened if I hadn't prayed.

About four hours later, I think, I was wheeled back into my room. I saw Rick's mom and she told me that my dad had arrived. I felt relieved. I spent a few minutes with the family, but I was still so groggy, that they left and let me sleep. Rick stayed with me. The girls would come up tomorrow.

After a couple hours, Rick said he was going to go home and get some sleep. This had been stressful for him, too. I begged him not to go. "Please, stay. I'm not feeling good. I can't breathe."

Around 7:00 p.m., I started experiencing severe discomfort and a strong choking sensation. The resident doctor checked my oxygen level and the incision at my neck. He tried to assure me this was normal after a radical neck operation. They had gone in through the front of my neck and there was swelling. It would go down. "Don't worry." But, it did not go away. It just kept getting worse.

I remember gasping. I had a hard neck collar on, to keep the neck stable. Because of the fragility of the spinal cord and the close proximity of it to the surgery, it was very important to keep everything still for several days. I was gagging. I must have looked an awful sight.

I looked down at Rick for what I thought would be the last time. I reached my hand out and just mouthed the words, "I love you." I was thinking, "I love you. You've been a wonderful husband. This is it. Take care of my girls for me. I don't want to die! I'm dying!" I guess I turned blue and fell back on the bed.

Rick thought I had died. He ran into the hall, screaming, "Code Blue, Code Red, somebody, HELP!" The nurses and doctor came running. I had gone into respiratory arrest. Rick was escorted, against his wishes, out into the hallway. He said he just started shouting the name of Jesus. One of the nurses came and asked if he was all right. "No!" he said, "but I'm talking to the One who can make it all right." She probably thought he was losing it and left him alone. But, he was touching the throne of God.

Through the grace of God and "divine intervention", as one nurse later told me, a breathing tube was inserted and I was resuscitated. I was then attached to a breathing machine because I was not breathing on my own.

The neurosurgeon was called. This was another "intervention". It was Saturday, and the doctor had left and gone to a party with his wife. He was paged at the party. Thankfully, he had not been drinking and was able to drive to the hospital within the hour. He ordered an X-ray to be done right there in the room, to try and determine exactly what was happening. An artery had been cut! I was bleeding to death. There was a blood clot the size of a plum. A second emergency surgery would have to be done immediately.

As I drew my last breath that Saturday night, I realized how close eternity is. I thought of my mother who had died when I was fifteen and I cried out to God, (in my subconscious) "Please don't take me away from my three little girls, like my mother who was taken so soon." I was ready to meet my Savior, but did not feel done on this earth yet. I wanted to recover. My plea would be granted.

Around midnight, they wheeled me into the operating room and started the second surgery, being very careful not to disrupt anything done from the previous surgery, or to injure the spinal cord. They capped the artery and removed the blood clot. I was then taken to Intensive Care and hooked up to life support, breathing machine, and all sorts of monitors. My condition would be critical for the next few hours.

Someone asked me if I had seen the "bright light". I did,

but I think it was the operating room light. I must have come to for just a second before the anesthesiologist put me "back under". I really don't remember anything for the next several hours and even days. Rick has filled me in a lot.

Daddy was at home with the girls and did not know of the crisis. Around 5:00 a.m., after Rick was convinced that I was stable and the nurses were watching me, he went home. (Remember, he hadn't slept for twenty four hours.)
He went into the bedroom where Daddy was sleeping and gently woke him up. "Burt, there's been a crisis with Jennifer. She had to have a second surgery ." He went on to explain what happened.

Daddy got ready and came to the hospital. Rick showered and went to bed for a little while. I remember waking up around 7:30 a.m. Sunday morning. I opened my eyes and saw my Daddy standing there, looking so worried. I realized something had gone wrong but I didn't know exactly what. I couldn't talk because of all the breathing tubes, up my nose, down my throat, and wires everywhere. I motioned for something to write with. "What happened to me?", I scribbled. Daddy explained, very briefly, so as not to worry me, I'm sure. "You'll be all right", he said. But I could see the concern in his face. "Just rest", he said, as he held my hand. So I did.

Later, Rick brought the girls up. I remember thinking how I wished I had said more to my mother when she died. I really didn't know if I was going to make it and I wanted to see my girls. They came into the Intensive Care room stepping ever so gently and looking so stunned. I will never forget their little faces. I wrote to them that I loved them. They prayed for me and then left.

After about three days, I was taken out of Intensive Care and moved to a regular room. I was still having that choking sensation and had to have a couple more X-rays to make sure the artery was still capped. The doctor said it was seeping a little bit, but that would subside. I felt like I was fighting for my life. I was having trouble with high fever, nightmares, not to mention, the pain from the hip incision and the neck incisions. I had a hard neck collar on and could hardly move. I had to turn my whole body, to turn my head.

Finally, on about the seventh day, my fever broke and I had a tremendous sense of peace that God was in control. I was going to make it. I'll admit, I did not have this peace at first. It was a very frightening time. I probably should have reflected on past milestones, but when you're in the midst of the battle, it can be hard to put things in perspective.

Milestone:
Realizing that a crisis can bring out the best and the worst in us. It is very important to trust God during these times based on faith not feelings. Remember, face to Faith. Standing on the promises because He tells me to , not always because I feel confident. Faith, "the substance of things hoped for, the evidence of things NOT seen".

After ten days I was allowed to go home. The prognosis was good, but recovery would take three months. I was not allowed to lift anything. Not even an empty laundry basket. I could not unload the dishwasher. Normally, this might sound like a vacation, but I realized I was more independent than I thought and I had already been in bed for a month. The prospect of three more months was hard to deal with.

My precious Daddy was so good. He took care of the girls, although I was informed that he "did not do hair". He fixed things around the house, cleaned, took the girls out for little outings, which really helped them stay positive.

The churches in the area were terrific. They brought in meals, house cleaners, flowers, cards, and anything we needed. Daddy would get the dinners on and the girls would pitch in too. It was definitely a special bonding time in our family.

My wonderful husband Rick was also very precious to me. After Daddy left, Rick took over and did EVERYTHING. All I could do was lay in my bed or sit in a chair.
Walking was difficult for about three weeks. Rick even gave me a bell to ring if I needed anything. (I'd like to use that bell now, but nobody responds, ha!) Rick did laundry, dishes, and he even did the girls' hair! He put up with my emotional roller coaster ride as well as my physical limitations for quite some time. He prayed with me often and was constantly encouraging me. He was my soulmate!

But it was still difficult. I was an active wife and mother, so it was almost inconceivable that I would be in bed or very limited in activity for three months. Yet, in the weeks that followed I realized there was a lot I could do. I could pray, read the Word, give someone a call of encouragement, (I was on the phone a lot), and grow in the Lord.

I was in the recovery process. I needed many things on my road to recovery - prayer, rest, and a gradual return to routine. God's Word and the support and prayers of family and friends helped me immensely.

Milestone:

Many of us go through experiences in our lives that require a recovery period. What we do in the recovery process is up to us. We can try to turn and run, perhaps too fast, and end up falling; or we can stand with arms outstretched reaching for God's hand that is extended to pull us through.

Though we don't understand each circumstance, God is in control. We have to pace ourselves and respect the healing process. Time heals. With time scars fade, pains go away and strength is regained.

It has now been three and one half years since that surgery. I guess you could say my life is back to "normal".

The surgery was successful. I am limited in a few things like: I can't ride roller coasters, I can't jump on the trampoline with my girls, I can't do high impact aerobics; not that I did any of these things with much regularity before the injury either. I struggle with Migraine headaches as a result of the pressure on the disc below the bone fusion.

What I can do, is live my life with enthusiasm, energy, and all of my limbs functioning like any other "thirty something" individual. I'm not as young as I used to be but with Grandma as my role model, my best days are still ahead.

Someone once quoted the following statement to me:

"Life is 10% what happens to you and 90% how you respond to what happens".

As I look back on those four months in bed, I step forward every day with a greater appreciation for my physical ability to run the vacuum cleaner, to load the dishwasher, to carry the "overflowing" laundry basket up and down the stairs, and to experience my daughters' growth as they prepare to leave the nest.

It may sound trite, but it's the valleys that make us appreciate the mountain tops. It took the serious to help me stop and appreciate the simple. So many times we take our lives for granted. We take our health for granted. We begrudge the monotony of our routines. But we grow only as each cycle is completed. It is a routine of nature.

If Jesus could still a storm on the sea of Galilee, then I trust Him to speak "peace" to my storms as they come along. Because of the "hail stones", I conquered a few more milestones, stepping forward on each one. You can too!

CHAPTER 16

Jacklyn - The Little Missionary

My firstborn daughter. From the time I was pregnant and dreaming about what this baby would look like, I began to know her. I didn't know if it would be a boy or a girl, but I had seen the baby in a dream. A beautiful, Italian baby, with lots of long, black hair. If it was a girl, her name would be Jacklyn Tennille. Jacklyn, because of Mother and Tennille, because I like the name. We would call her Tennille.

But, from the second she was born, Rick started calling her "Jacklyn". He had never met my mother and didn't really know who she had been, but he knew Jacklyn was going to be her namesake.

She looked exactly like some of Mother's baby pictures. The big, brown eyes, long, black hair, olive skin (Mother's came from German roots, Jacklyn's from German and Italian). How I wished Mother could have been there.

Jacklyn Tennille was a beautiful baby, born after 17 hours of labor, and two trips for false labor as well. She didn't even hardly cry. Matter of fact, I guess she was like THE Perfect Baby! She would eat, sleep four hours, eat, sleep four hours, AND she slept through the night almost immediately. She was a happy and contented baby. She was easy! (It's probably a good thing she was first, because it made me look forward to having more just like her.)

Milestone:
Giving birth, especially for the first time, is the most awesome involvement in a miracle you could ever have. Having a husband to share that experience, is the most wonderful expression of two becoming one. Having Jacklyn was another dream fulfilled for me. Now, I would have a real baby doll to go to church with me.

There's a lot I could say about Jacklyn. She's a wonderful daughter, and at fourteen, she's becoming my sweet friend as well. She's been a 4.0, all A's student.

She told me very definitely at four years old, that she had Jesus in her heart and she just wanted to go to the altar to "get more of God".

At seven, she was baptized in water, took her first communion and received the baptism in the Holy Spirit. I was beginning to see that she was very serious about her relationship with God and she was learning how to fellowship with Him, herself.

From the time she was two years old until four years old, we were on the evangelistic field. She was in church almost every single night. She loved it! She loved meeting people, she loved singing on the platform with her Mom, "I'm Yours Lord", she loved traveling, hotels, lots of stops at McDonald's. She was still easy. Sometimes I wonder if (actually I know) God was preparing her even then, for the calling He would place on her life.

When she was in the fourth grade, she had to write a speech for school. It was the McDonald's "When I Grow Up" speech contest and it involved schools all over Michigan. When she came to me to read the rough draft of what she had already written, I wanted to cry. My baby had a dream. She wanted (still wants) to be a Missionary to Italy.

We were Pastoring in Grand Rapids at the time, and she had been talking to every missionary that came to our church. In fourth grade, she already knew about language school, preliminary time on the field, and how she was going to incorporate all of this into her four years of college, at home and abroad, so that by the time she graduated from college, she would already have her "base" set up in Italy and would be ready to start working.

The following is a copy of her speech:

"WHEN I GROW UP, I WANT TO BE A MISSIONARY!"

Just imagine people everywhere wanting food, needing clothing, looking for shelter, reaching out. Then, they see me and I see them, and I reach out, because reaching out is what being a Missionary is all about.

Hello, my name is Jacklyn Pasquale, and I want to be a Missionary when I grow up. I first dreamed I wanted to be a Missionary when I was in church, sitting on the front row, listening to my dad, preaching about Missionaries. He said that the people all over the world are wanting to learn about Jesus. Then God spoke to me and said, "Jacklyn, I want you to go to Italy!" I just sat there and thought about that. Then I said to myself, "why does God want me to do this job?" Maybe it's because I'm Italian, or maybe it's because I love pasta, or maybe it's just because I love people. Well, one thing I know for sure, I have dreamed of it ever since.

I chose this career because God called me to do

so, and also because I like telling people about Jesus. I care about people, and through this job, maybe I can help them.

My grandfather is my role model. I look at him and think, "Someday, that's what I'm going to be." He quit his regular job to go to a different country every month, and build churches for people who don't have them.

I will achieve this goal by going to college to learn about different cultures and people, and how to react to them. I will take language classes to help improve my communication skills and would hope to participate in a student exchange program.

I have to be flexible, kindhearted, selfless, I won't have time to worry about myself, compassionate, creative, assertive, and for sure, Bold! Right now I am looking forward to becoming a Missionary and I will continue to pray each day until I fulfill my dream.

This career is about teaching God's love, showing God's love through your actions, teaching about His word, and training others to succeed.

I will preach and teach to people in Italy about God's love. I will help organize getting homes for the homeless, dinners for the poor and needy, arrange for medical staff to come and work in a clinic for the sick, operate a school for the children, and have exciting services to bring the gospel to other people.

From the time I was four years old, standing at the bottom of the Eiffel Tower in Paris, France, 'till now, until the day I'm standing on the soil of Italy; I have, I do, and I always will care about sharing my blessings as an American, and my freedom to worship my Lord freely with others, in every way I can!"

She won out of her school, her district and placed 4th in

our region. The following year, we moved to the Walled Lake School district and she did the same speech again, with some modifications and improvements. She won again! All the way to the top ten out of about 150 schools in many different districts in the metro Detroit area. (Remember, this was public school, she was nine years old and she was already spreading the Light!)

Another accomplishment of Jacklyn's was being published in a Nationally circulated Christian magazine, called the Pentecostal Evangel:

"IF I COULD GIVE THE WORLD A GIFT"
by Jacklyn Pasquale

A homeless child
Alone, hungry
Friendship
A trip to McDonald's

A widowed mother
Poor, lonely
A place to work
A card, a phone call

Juveniles in Trouble
Afraid, desperate
A trustworthy judge
A loving mentor

An AIDS victim
Worried, diseased
Hope for tomorrow
A cure for today

Fighting nations
Prejudice, destruction
All men created equal
Unconditional love

Me, myself
What I can give
Faithful prayers
My life extended.

At twelve years old, after three years in the Missionettes ministry, Jacklyn graduated as an Honor Star. She scored one less than perfect on her District test and went on to compete in a State competition for the Michigan District. She was crowned the Princess of the Michigan District, the highest honor in our state. I couldn't have been more proud. She had done something I had never been able to do as a child and because of it, her knowledge of God's word, and her understanding of God's plan for her life was sealed in her mind as well as her heart. I think she knew more about her faith than many grown-ups.

Milestone:

Rejoicing in the accomplishments of our children is thrilling. I can just barely imagine how Father God must rejoice when His children accomplish the goals He has for them. I want to be that kind of child to Father God and Jacklyn was setting an example for me. Kids teach parents, too, sometimes.

Her transition to Junior High in the seventh grade was somewhat difficult. Not with her grades, she received many academic awards that year. But, socially. Junior Highers are very cliquish and Jacklyn had made everybody aware of her desire to Stand Up for God. Peer pressure was something she just didn't conform to.

With her dad in District work now, we were attending a lot of different churches with him and she was not really getting settled in a youth group. She was lonely at school. She still loved the ministry and church opportunities, but her female emotions were kicking in. Easy? Well, let's just say, normal. After fourteen years, I guess a little bit of normal was okay.

The summer after her seventh grade year, she competed in a National talent competition. She entered two categories, Vocal Solo, and Short Sermon. Her passion for ministry skills was evident in her entries. She won the State Merit award for Short Sermon and received Superiors in both categories all the way to National, including the Final Finals. She was ministering!

In September, she started back to school in the eighth grade. Her last year of Junior High. We had all been praying that God would give her some Christian friends at school this year. We/she needed God to obviously answer this prayer.

Another thing was going on at this same time. I had been diagnosed with "Dengue Fever". I had gotten it from a mosquito bite in the Philippines that summer. My body temperature would go crazy, hot, then cold, sweats, and chills. I was literally dingy. I couldn't think straight, everything seemed blurry and I was constantly on the edge of passing out if I got up.

It was Friday and I had been in and out of the hospital, just laying there in bed. Rick was home because it was his day off. The phone rang. Rick answered it, spoke just a few minutes and then hung up. Jacklyn had been "injured" and he had to go to school to get her. I didn't know what was going on. I just kind of thought she must have gotten hurt in gym. Probably, no big deal.

When Rick got to the school, he found out that Jacklyn had been beaten up. The side of her face was swollen and bruised. He was shocked! How could this be? School had only been in session for two weeks. What could Jacklyn have done to provoke this kind of anger from someone? Who did it? What happened?

After some discussion, he found out that it had happened between classes, when all the 800 students are passing quickly to get to their next class. Obviously, the teachers were still in their classrooms and not there in the hall to protect. I never thought they needed protection. (Not in this nice suburban neighborhood, where almost all the parents came to almost all the events. This was a family community)

Jacklyn had evidently, accidentally, bumped into the wrong girl in passing. This girl, Nikki, threw her books on the floor and started pounding Jacklyn's face with her fist. Then she took Jacklyn's head and crashed it into the lockers, about six times. Jacklyn raised her two hands, flat across her face to try to protect herself from the blows. Then, it was over. Nikki took off and left Jacklyn standing there crying. Jacklyn and a friend went immediately to the office to tell and show that she had been beaten up.

What happened next was unbelievable! Jacklyn was suspended! The school has a policy that ANY students involved in a fight would be suspended. This was to deter kids from getting in fights. Jacklyn was suspended for one day, Nikki for two. Rick was furious when he heard. The assistant principle basically said, "Mr. Pasquale, your daughter got beat up in a fight and she is being suspended. You can take her home now." Rick, (who strongly believes in letting our Christian kids be on public school campuses to keep The Light shining), replied, "You're making a big mistake, this may be the last time you ever see my daughter." And then, they came home.

When I saw Jacklyn, I thought something was wrong with

my vision. I was trying to focus. She laid on the bed beside me and cried. I cried and Rick cried. How could God have let this happen? We prayed for friendship and we got a fight. Not only that, she had gotten suspended for getting beat up!

I was not so dingy, that I couldn't feel. I was furious! She would never go back to public school, we'd find a good Christian school and transfer her on Monday. It's our job to protect our children, right?

Then we started talking. Over the weekend, after we had calmed down, a very little bit, we started talking. We realized Jacklyn needed to be involved in this decision, what did she want to do? What was she thinking?

The first thing on the list was to get this suspension deal corrected. We had a meeting with the principal and the assistant principal and the counselor. We got the school district's Code of Conduct book. There was nothing in there that said Jacklyn should have been suspended, in fact, there were other options of punishment they could have given. Suspension was the maximum punishment! We reminded them of Jacklyn's incredible academic and social record. We reminded them of all the outstanding reports from all of her teachers. We reminded them of her good citizenship awards. This child was not a fighter! She was a lover of souls, but they wouldn't understand that.

After meeting with the Principal, Assistant Principal and Counselor, it was decided by them, that they would have to think about all that we had said and get back to us. Within a couple days, the Principal called to say they had made a mistake. Jacklyn should not have been suspended. They were sorry. WOW! He also put this in writing, revoking the suspension, and sent a letter to all of her teacher as well, explaining their mistake, and Jacklyn's innocence. The principal told us that he needed more students like Jacklyn in this school, and would we please consider leaving her there.

It was the hardest thing in my parenting, so far, to not just want to take her and hide her away from all the bad, to protect her in my way. But God reminded us that she is HIS, His little sparrow, who He is watching after.

Finally, Rick and Jacklyn sat on the side of her bed and tried to come to some decision. Would she return to this public school campus and be at risk, or would we take her out and put her in a safe, private, Christian school? (I know there are times when Christian school is best or even home schooling. Each person must decide for their children based on factors of community, curriculum, and administrations' receptiveness to Christians in the public school.) But, in this case, after counseling with the Pastor of the church we were attending, we felt Jacklyn should have a say in what she felt most comfortable with. My precious twelve year old, sat on the side of the bed, and said to her dad, "I can not leave my mission field. If God has called me to be a missionary, then how will I ever minister on foreign soil, if I can't minister right here at home. That girl may never know forgiveness, if I don't go back to school and forgive her. I have to go back." With both of them crying, the decision was made. Jacklyn returned to her school.

As a result, two girls, later that month, came with Jacklyn to church and gave their lives to Christ. One of these girls, who comes from a divorce situation, continues to go with us to church every week and is growing rapidly in the Lord. The girl who beat her up has now become her "protector" at school. When other kids try to tease or ridicule Jacklyn, this girl will say, "Leave her alone, she's cool." She even told Jacklyn she was sorry and was glad that Jacklyn had shown kindness to her. At this time, we are still praying for her, that God will open the right door for Jacklyn to bring her to the Lord. My little missionary.

Milestone:
Sometimes it is so hard to really give our kids to the Lord. I was thinking, "God, you can have her when she's grown, but she's just a kid, not now." But God is so faithful! When we let Him have them, He does more with their hearts and attitudes than we could do in a thousand conversations with them. He is the ultimate parental authority and we as His children, must trust Him with ALL our lives.

At this time, Jacklyn is now a freshman in high school. That's a whole other story. I never thought I would be old enough to have a daughter wearing my clothes and driving my car. Again, just another step down the path; letting go, again. I've decided it's all part of the continuum.

She remains a 4.0 student, who consistently goes the extra mile to put forth her best work. I guess Rick's intolerance of mediocrity has been passed on to her. She approaches her spiritual life the same way and loves God, loves souls, and still wants to be a missionary to Italy. She weeps over the indifference of her Christian friends and rejoices when God does something awesome in anybody's life. She is one of my three "pride and joys".

She recently won a National Speaking Competition and is truly wise beyond her years. She has been a constant source of joy in our lives.

She is fifteen, beautiful, long, dark hair, big brown eyes, slender, graceful and mostly joyful and "perky". But, she is normal.

She's sensitive, emotional, sometimes moody, always on the phone, and a perfectionist - therefore, sometimes a slowpoke. She even rolls her eyes up in her head at me and mocks me when I don't get a joke or fail to comprehend her college level math assignments. She's definitely ahead of her time and sometimes ahead of mine.

Milestone:
Kids are human too. No matter what their academic status or social maturity, they must be allowed to have their childhood. There is a fine balance between pushing them towards excellence and giving them the space for imperfections. Raising children is God's way of allowing us as parents, to practice the fruits of mercy and tolerance. The four L's: Love, laughter, listening, and loyalty. A time for all seasons and sometimes, all seasons in one time. What a juggling act.

Jacklyn will graduate, Lord willing, in the class of 2000. Her class will lead us into the next millennium. Will she be up to the task? Will we, as parents, have done our best for her? All I know, is that with God, "all things are possible". Without God, we're allowing open territory for her data bank to be filled by unchaperoned, morality; which in this day, means no morality. It's not worth the risk. I want to give her all of the helps she could possibly need, spiritual, emotional, physical, etc. If I don't give her the knowledge of what God can do, I cause the handicap in her life. "Train up a child in the way they should go, and when they grow up, they will know what is right and do it." (paraphrased)

CHAPTER 17

Jessica Danielle - Energy in Motion!

As stated in a previous chapter, Jessica was born shortly after Todd's accident, on December 13, 1984. She was the traveling baby. We continued to minister on the evangelistic field and would take her to services in a "Moses" basket and she would usually sleep right through the service. But as soon as the social activities started, like eating in the restaurant, she would be awake and demanding my attention. It wasn't hard to lose my pregnancy weight. I never got to eat. (Well, almost never.)

Jessica was my only child to be born by Cesarean section. She was in a footling breech position, otherwise known as the splits, and it was the safest way to deliver.

Another Daddy's girl. I remember Rick going with her to the baby nursery, just minutes after she was born. When they rolled me out of recovery, past the nursery, and towards my room, I looked over and saw Rick, in his hospital robe, sitting in a rocking chair, holding a tiny bundle in a pink blanket. There was such pride and joy on his face, I knew he was happy. It was a very special memory. To this day, the two of them remain especially close. Granted, she is the little tomboy and tries to take her dad on the basketball court whenever possible. Actually, all my girls have a great relationship with their father, but this chapter is about Jessica.

Jessica has always been our social butterfly. When she was in the womb, we prayed for a healthy, happy, outgoing baby. I knew that in the ministry, they would be around a lot of people and I didn't want her to be a "clingy" baby. Now, I wish she would "cling" a little more. Needless to say, she is independent. I use to tell her she was half Italian and half Texan. She recently informed me that Texan is NOT a nationality, and she was born in Ann Arbor, Michigan and she is a Michigander. How delightful when our children discover who they are and they're happy with the discovery.

When Jessica was in the fourth grade, she was given a writing assignment at Halloween time. The teacher would later tell us that most of the assignments turned in would be filled with bloody, gorey, details, based on all of the scary movies kids were seeing at that time of year. The teacher didn't especially like the assignment, but it was part of the curriculum ordered by the school board. The children had read a story about a little boy, named Devon. He was going through the woods and got lost. He came upon an old, abandoned house with a brass door. He went up to the door. ....

Now, the children were to write a conclusion to the story. What did Devon find beyond the door? Jessica made a cover for her story with a piece of construction paper, folded like a book. On the cover, was a house with a brass door that opened. There was an angel standing by the door. This is what Jessica wrote:

"As he looked into the room, Devon saw a gate made of pearls. He looked through the gate and he saw streets of gold and 1,000 story mansions. When he looked again he saw the holy city suspended like a cube. He looked and looked and in God's glory he saw the Master, the Savior, King of all Kings, the Bread

of Life, the Living Water. He saw GOD! God is as big as 1,000 giants put together. Suddenly Devon saw an angel, it was Gabriel.

Gabriel said unto him, "If you want to enter, you must ask Jesus to come into your heart." Devon said, "All right." So they bowed their heads and Devon repeated after Gabriel. "Amen" they said together.

Devon was so happy that he had invited God into his heart. He went in and talked to God. God said "Devon it is time for church". Devon said "Okay, let's go." When they got there Devon said a prayer, it goes like this. "My father which art in Heaven, hallowed be thy name, thy kingdom come, thy work be done on earth as it is in Heaven. Give us this day our daily bread and forgive us our debts as we forgive our debtors. And lead us not into temptation, but deliver us from evil. For thine is the kingdom, the power, and the glory forever, Amen."

Devon said, "Will you please tell my mom I'm okay and that Heaven is a wonderful place, filled with glory and grace, with streets of gold and gates of pearls, and marvelous mansions! The End"

As the teacher shared Jessica's story with Rick and I at a Parent/Teacher conference, we began to cry. The teacher cried. Her student teacher was crying. The teacher told us she had shared the story with the school counselor and she cried. She had shared it with the principal and the other fourth grade teachers and some of the students and they had all been deeply moved by this story. She said it was the most incredible piece of writing a student had ever turned in to her.

Rick and I just sat there and could barely explain that God was very real to Jessica. Obviously, she had taken HIM personally. The teacher agreed and assured us that we had a very special child.

We walked out of that school on Cloud Nine. All of the training, all of the church involvements, all of the prayers had paid off. Jessica knew what she believed and she had shared it, at age nine, in PUBLIC SCHOOL! Now, that was cool!

Milestone:

Our children are never too young to begin learning God's plan for their lives. They are not too young to understand eternity or too young to make choices affecting their eternity. We MUST give children the opportunity to be introduced to God and His great plans and then allow them to make an educated choice about whom they will serve. "Bring up a child in the way he should go, and when he is old, he will not depart from it." Our society needs values and children need parents with values to teach them. We can ALL "Bloom where we're planted", no matter the age.

The most recent memory I have of something special in Jessica's life is what happened to her this summer. We had taken 341 students to the Atlanta Olympics for ministry outreach. It was Jessica's dream to attend one of the gymnastic competitions. Remember, in the splits, in the womb and still "splitting" at age eleven. With the popularity of gymnastics, tickets were outrageous in price and almost impossible to purchase. But, she had a dream.

We were on the Marta rail system, on our way to downtown Atlanta to do some ministry. Jessica was sitting by an older man and glanced down and noticed he was holding a gymnastics' ticket.

With her big brown eyes and inquisitive smile, she looked up at him and said, "Wow, you have a gymnastics ticket.

Could I just *look* at it."

He obliged, and they struck up a conversation and my little social butterfly began to tell this stranger all about her gymnastics "career and ambitions".

"You know what?" the man said, "You can just have that ticket." I think she about bounced off that Marta and she definitely bounced over to where I was sitting, through the crowd, and stuffed the ticket in my face. "Look, Mom, that man gave me this gymnastic ticket. You have to take me. Now!!"

I looked down and saw the price, $260 and realized the improbability of this. I went to the man and asked him if he was sure, did he want any money for the ticket. (I prayed he'd say no, because I sure didn't have $260). He told me that it was an extra ticket, they were already thirty minutes late, and it wouldn't be used, so she could just have it as a keepsake.

Well, I got excited along with Jessica, and we decided to try to make it to the coliseum and see if there was still time for her to catch even a few minutes of competition. As we jumped off the Marta, and boarded another one headed for gymnastics, I began to think. "How could I let this eleven year old child go into that huge arena without me? How would she find me afterwards in that massive crowd of over 75,000 people? What if she went to the wrong exit? How could I let her do this? How could I not let her have her dream fulfilled. This was a $260/free gift, how could we not take advantage of it? I started praying.

As we got off the Marta and headed down the sidewalk, I started looking for "scalpers". A man came up to us and offered us a $260 ticket. Of course, I said No and kept walking.

The man ran after us and said, "Lady, make me an offer." I said, "$20" He thought I was crazy and frankly, so did I. But the next thing I knew, he was at my side again, saying

Okay, $20.

This was the second miracle in this chain of events. We were IN, TOGETHER!

Now, where would these two seats be?

When God does something, He does it right! Our tickets were in the same section, only four rows apart. Jessica was never out of my sight. AND, they were only about four or five rows from the main floor. She could see every gymnast, every drop of sweat, every grimace and every expression of joy when a move was made. It was totally awesome!

Afterwards, we were so appreciative of the man's generosity, we asked if we could take his picture with Jessica. You see, they had ended up sitting by each other, because he had used his other tickets.

As we were talking, he explained to us why he had the extra ticket. He and his wife had purchased four tickets so that they could bring their two sons on a vacation in celebration of the boys, both, graduating from college. It was to be their last big family event, before the boys got on with their adult lives. Just weeks before Atlanta, his wife had died of cancer, and the trip had become bittersweet.

The Lord opened up this opportunity for us to encourage this man and his sons. We shared of God's faithfulness in getting us through Mother's death, of how God had helped my Daddy rebuild his life and restored hope and joy to him. The man reflected on hearing of God's love as a child and said Jessica had brought a ray of hope for joy back to his life. He said, it was time to give God a chance to restore some joy to him.

Two different people, an eleven year old girl with dreams of a future and a fifty-five year old man with memories of the past. Merged together, by the hand of God, and both were touched by a God who knows and understands our deepest longings.

Milestone:
Sometimes, we feel like an insignificant speck. Could God really care about our little wishes and dreams? YES! We are his sparrows. He knows when we fall and when we fly and He is there at all times. He grants our desires on a level that enables us to see God right where we're at and He meets our needs in the most unexpected ways. I'm sure Peter never expected to walk on water. I'm sure Mary never expected to have a baby without a husband. I'm sure the people never expected to see Lazarus after he was put in that tomb. I'm sure the disciples never expected to talk with the resurrected Lord. But, God goes beyond our highest expectations. We can't designate our miracle specifications. If we could, it wouldn't be a miracle. We must be on the lookout for God to do the unexpected and receive our miracles. Jessica got hers and so did the stranger with the gymnastic ticket. God is no respector of persons.

Jessica is a joy and it is our prayer that people will see it is the LIGHT within her that makes her so bright. "By this, shall all men know that ye are my disciples, if ye have love for one another." Our little social butterfly reached out to a man and helped him reach back to God.

CHAPTER 18

Ericka Jane - Parenting 101

Oh boy! Where do I begin? Named after her father, E-Rick-A, and after my preacher, grandmother, Jane.

At three years old, she told a waitress, "I'm going to be a ballerina - preacher when I grow up." I'm not quite sure how to address this dream of hers. However, at eight years old, her dreams are still evolving. She wants to be a cheerleader now. That's what a preacher is. Someone who roots for their team and tries to get the fans to do the same. And to do it with excitement!

Excitement. That's the word. Never a dull moment with Ericka or Rickie, as she is sometimes called. This child has caused me to read every book ever written on parenting and the strong-willed child, TWICE!

At two, I thought I might have to send her away to military school. She flooded the church bathroom with ten gallons of water; she was just trying to help "Keen the sink, mommy."

She came into the secretary's office, while my husband - Senior Pastor husband, his business guest, and the youth pastor were all standing there. One problem, she was stark naked. "I all wet, Mommy."

She dusted the entire nursery, all of herself, her friend, and all of the toys with baby powder and looked like a guilty ghost, when I walked in on her, giving a friend a tour of the church. "I make babies smell dood, Mommy."

She wrote all over my devotional Bible, along with the white, living room rug, with an orange highlighter. "I do 'votions (devotions), like you, Mommy."

She took my red lipstick and got it all over my white wool suit, which I had carelessly left hanging over her rocking chair, (we shared a closet at that time). I have to stop for a minute.

Milestone:
Always hang up your clothes when you take them off.

Anyway, the red lipstick was being used by my precious Ericka to draw a happy face on her three foot, stuffed caterpillar. "I make her happy, Mommy." (Her, being the caterpillar; I was not the happy one in the room.)

But, life goes on and they mature. We survived the Terrific Two's. THE GRACE OF GOD IS SUFFICIENT! And she experienced the grace of God, along with the wrath of Mom.

But I do have other memories of Ericka. One very special little girl with a heart for others.

When my dad was diagnosed with cancer and we thought we might lose him, she prayed fervently, every night for three months that God would touch those lymphs. He did!

After hearing of Papa's miracle, Ericka diligently thanked God, every night for almost three months for answering her prayer. At six years old, she had a Friend in Heaven and she knew it.

Milestone:
Jesus said, "Let the little children come to me?" He said, "a child shall lead them". We must give our children the opportunity to experience God for themselves. You don't have to be an adult to understand God. You don't have to be a child to experience His "parenting". God has taught me so much through this third, born gift. And believe me, it is a never ending, educational experience.

Ericka is a prayer warrior. She knows how to pray. She should, she has to pray for repentance quite often. She, too, is very normal.

When she was about seven years old, it seemed like she was going through the Terrible Two's again. She was getting in trouble a lot. It seemed like all I ever did was spank her. So, like any good mother, I started to give up and give in. It was just less noisy that way.

Finally, after one evening of whining and disobeying, Rick reminded me that I needed to be more consistent. "You can't give in to her.", he told me.

So, the next day when she disobeyed, I very calmly told her, "You will get a spanking if you do not obey me." She made the choice to disobey and I made the choice to be consistent.

"Ericka," I said, "Bend over, you're getting a spanking." I was so calm and feeling very in control of myself, not frustrated, just following through.

"No, No!" she screamed, "You can't spank me. You always spank me."

"I know, Ericka, spankings teach you to obey."

"Well!," she cried, "these spankings aren't working."

"Ericka," I said, "I have to spank you, the Bible says sometimes children need to be spanked."

"The Bible says?", she cried, "THEN THE BIBLE'S

WRONG."

We went on to have a discussion about "Sparing the rod and spoiling the child", about "children, obey your parents", and about God's word and how we don't always like what it says. But, it's for our own good. And, we talked about how much I love her and other types of discipline that were available.

Maybe she was right. Spanking doesn't always work. But there does need to be a consequence for wrong behavior. It is a fact of life and if we don't teach our children that when they are young, they will be in for a big shock when they become adults. Discipline is necessary for holding down jobs, dealing with unpleasant people and so much of life's little routines.

Milestone:
The athlete knows discipline, his coach makes sure of that. But, when his team wins the championship, he understands the discipline. Someday, we're going to win the FINAL Championship and I want to make sure my kids are on the winning team.

One time when we were on vacation, Ericka decided that she was tired of being called Ericka. She was tired of being called "Janie", her nickname. As we were driving to the Hotel Boulevard, she looked out the window, declaring she was changing her name to......... her eyes lit up and she said, "I'm changing my name to Marriot." Jessica looked at her and said, "More like Mary Rotten". For the rest of the vacation, Ericka only responded to her new name, Marriot.

Milestone:
You may not like your name now, or who you are, but if you take on the name of Jesus Christ, one day, you're going to get a new name and it will be written in the Lamb's Book of Life and your eternal destiny will be secure.

Another more recent story: Ericka was recently having a little trouble giving all the details in TRUE statements. And, this was getting on my last nerve. Finally, I said, "You have about five seconds to remember exactly what happened." She thought for a few minutes, grabbed the sides of her head with both hands, as if trying to shake that memory loose in there. Suddenly, she replied, "Oh, Oh, I know, I just had the wrong memory! Now I remember." Yes, we had a long discussion on one of the ten commandments that says, "Thou shall not bear false witness."

Milestone:
Discipline is a necessity of life. I wonder how many times the Lord would like us to recite the Ten Commandments. Forgive and it shall be forgiven you. Just like little children, we forget, we fail, sometimes we even forsake. But like the loving parent, He forgives, He restores us in to right relationship and He never stops loving us.

During the writing of this book, Ericka has really been growing in the Lord. Just recently, she was at an altar of prayer, seeking God and just praising Him. She looked at me and said, "I don't think I can get up." I said, "Well, I guess God's not done with you yet." She smiled and responded, "Oh, GOOD!" and she just kept praising the Lord.

Milestone:
Wouldn't it be wonderful, if we all approached God that way, "Oh, Good, God's not done yet." And we just keep keeping on.

Ericka is in the third grade and has not had many writing assignments up to this point. Less she feel neglected, I asked her to write me something about her family so I could put it in her chapter.

This is what she wrote one morning in November, 1996:

"My mom is sweet
My dad is cool
And I think they really rool!
My sister Jess is the best!
My sister Jack has black hair
It's so strong it does not tair.
All together were like bair famlys becus
Were so loving and so snugling
Love is special. Love is kind
We shar it with other kinds
becus Jesus rains and is comming back another day
He's allways neer He's never away!
And We never ever forget to pray!!"

Well, spelling may be her weak subject, but she knows what she thinks and I'm happy with her thoughts.

Ericka makes us laugh. She's sensitive and sensational! And she's often unexplainable. I love her!

CHAPTER 19

Losing Daddy? - Gaining a Miracle

I told you in an earlier chapter, that there was one more memory of Daddy that would require an entire chapter. Here it is.

It was the summer of 1994, I was in a phone booth in Moscow, Russia. We were there with about 100 students to plant a church. I was calling home to Tomball, Texas, to see how my girls were. They were staying with Papa-Burt and Grandma-Gena. My sister, Tiffanie, answered the phone.

"How is everything, Tiffanie?" I asked. She didn't answer. I called her name. I thought the reception must be bad, half way around the world.

Finally, she answered, "I can't tell you, you'll have to talk to Daddy." "What do you mean? Where is he?" I didn't know if something was wrong with the girls or what. Daddy wasn't available to come to the phone, I'd have to call back.

I pleaded with her, this was long distance, it's not easy to find a working phone in Russia, I might not be able to get another call out, WHAT IS IT? "Daddy has a tumor", Tiffanie finally said. I could tell she was crying. "It's malignant." Now, I was crying. I hadn't felt this helpless in years.

I wanted to hug my sister, talk to my daddy, hold my girls

and I was a million miles away.

I had to wait for seven days, when we finally arrived back home in the United States, to find out the details. I called as soon as we landed in New York. I couldn't wait until we got home to Michigan.

Daddy had bone cancer. Daddy had Lymphoma, two kinds. The prognosis was very grim. The first doctor told him he would probably have three months. He basically said, I can't treat it, you're in stage four, go home and die. (Some doctors have lost their compassion for individuals and forgotten that medicine was designed to heal. But God is the Healer who never forgets His mission.)

My dad went for a second opinion. This doctor basically told him, "Yes, you will probably die from this cancer, but I can treat you and try to give you a little extra time. This kind of cancer, in stage four can not be cured, but we can sometimes slow it down."

My dad went for a third opinion. Not in a hospital or medical center, but at an altar of prayer. He called us and we joined him in this third "consultation". No "answer" was given immediately, except one: HOPE! Whether God would chose to heal or not, it seemed as though we all had peace that He would see us through this crisis. Peace that passes understanding!

I remember sitting at youth camp that summer, watching our teenagers receive from the Lord and feeling so desperate myself. I was pleading with the Lord. I didn't want to lose my daddy. "You took my mother, God, please, don't take my daddy. I do not want to be parentless."

I had not shared these feelings with anyone, not even, Rick. About that time, the evangelist came over to me. He said, "Jennifer, the Lord has a word for you. He wants you to know that He will not leave you Fatherless. He is your Father and He holds your situation in the palm of His hand." God is so awesome!

Milestone:
God knows our deepest and innermost thoughts. Nothing is a secret to Him. When we are desperate, He delivers hope.

My dad began extensive Chemotherapy. The doctors and nurses told him it would make him even sicker, but they would try to counter act that with other medicines. It was tough. He got extremely tired, experienced severe bone and joint pain, and felt terrible a lot. But, he only got really nauseous one time. That was a miracle.

In December, we were at our Youth Convention. One of our youth pastors, called us up on stage and shared this burden with 3,000 teenagers. He told them, "We've got to pray for Jennifer's dad." And we prayed, they prayed, and Heaven listened.

Less than three weeks later, we got a call from my dad. He had been back to the doctor and things seemed to be getting worse. So, the doctor ordered more tests, bone marrow sampling, CAT scans, blood work. The results came back and she ordered more tests.

Why? The cancer was gone. There weren't dead cancer cells, there was just NO cancer cells. The cancer, the spots in the lymph system, everything, GONE! CURED! MIRACLE! The doctor couldn't explain it, so Daddy did. He told her, we had all been praying. And she told him, "I think Someone heard your prayers." Hallelujah!

I'll be honest. I almost couldn't believe my ears. My grandfather had died of bone cancer. I had seen my dad and he looked like he was dying. Once, I had flown down to be with him for one of his Chemo treatments. I didn't even recognize him at the airport, when he came to pick me up. But God ALWAYS sees beyond what we see and God had come through, again!

When we got the news, it spread throughout our state to all those teenagers who had prayed. They were ecstatic. God had done a miracle and they had been involved in it! What a faith builder for them. Many of them saw my dad later at a Talent competition and were thrilled to see a living miracle. One they had prayed for. God still does miracles!

Milestone:

God is sovereign. We can not demand He answer our prayers our way, but we must expect Him to answer according to His word. Does he cure cancer every time? No Why? I don't know. But I do know that we have not because we ask not. And I also know we must ask, according to His will, not ours. Sometimes, we are so careful to pray so as not to be disappointed. But this situation reminded me that I must pray expecting, and then accept whatever God designs.

I also am thankful that I still have my earthly father, but was reminded that God will be my father, no matter what the circumstances and He holds the circumstances. All I have to do is hold His hand. I might be tempted to let go, or get tired and loosen my grip, but HE NEVER LETS GO!

My daddy told me one day, during the awful chemo and side effects: "Today is tough, but I'm holding on 'till tomorrow."

And God spoke to me for Daddy: "You don't have to fight this. I (God) already fought the battle and I won. Just let Me take care of it and you rest and trust." We don't have to fight always, we just have to trust.

CHAPTER 20

My Hero

Where do I begin to describe the love of my life? How can I put into words all of the characteristics my darling husband has and how they have been so effective in bringing me down this sometimes "rocky" road.

I've already told you of our early days, but a lifetime of memories has happened in eighteen years. Memories that have truly been milestones in my life. Memories that have kept me going when things got dry, made me laugh when things were hard, and made me thankful when I had a tendency to take things for granted.

Rev. Rickie Daniel Pasquale, the big "40" as of August 13, 1997, is sometimes referred to as "Rocky", the strong Italian physical characteristics, most likely responsible for that description. He has always had a strong jaw, broad shoulders, and a great passion for life. His protective arms have surrounded me in comfort, compassion, and just plain fun.

To say he loves sports, would be a tremendous understatement. (The remote control has direct dial to any athletic event.) His body may be getting older, just a little bit, but his heart and soul will always be twenty years old.

I have followed him around the world, literally. I should probably say, he has taken me to the edges of the planet. What a journey?

As I look back on that week of prayer and fasting when I was sixteen years old, and the anticipation in my heart when I first laid eyes on what was to be the "answer to my prayer", I am overwhelmed with God's goodness. He went way beyond my expectations.

Milestone:

So many times we fail to pray, believing that God really cares about the desires of our hearts. But, if we would only take HIM literally at HIS word, and OBEY, His endless treasures could be ours. "Delight thyself also in the Lord; and he shall give thee the desires of thine heart. Commit thy way unto the Lord; trust also in him; and he shall bring IT to pass."
-Psalms 37: 4,5

Rick and I have had some outrageous moments together and walked through many milestones. I remember him at the birth of each child, always ecstatic, never for a moment disappointed that it was a girl. He was so gentle with them. He was also playful with them. Until one of them would spit up, then, they were all mine.

When Jacklyn was about three months old, she barely slobbered on him; he threw the pacifier across the room, held her up and away from him in the air, and yelled for me to come clean her up. He has a very weak stomach.

He is always right there whenever they have any kind of competition. Bible quiz, gymnastics, speech giving, Fine Arts (National Assemblies of God talent competition). Sometimes, his "coaching" from the sidelines can become a little nerve wracking, but everyone in the room knows he's rooting for his daughter and he's intense.

I told you he was passionate about everything in life. No

common complacency for this man, no mediocrity tolerated, everything done with excellence in mind.

He ALWAYS makes bedtime prayers with our girls a special occasion. He has been a wonderful spiritual leader in our home and brings balance to our lives.

I love to picture him laying on one of the girls' beds in some cotton shorts and a white T-shirt, spread across the whole bed, usually smashing the one underneath her covers already. The other two piled in around him, hanging over his shoulder or just kneeling by the bed at his feet. I'm usually standing or sitting on the last inch of mattress available, but we're all there.

He should feel like King of the Mountain, but he demonstrates complete loyalty to his clan. These times of prayer have come to be a wonderful opportunity to reflect on events of the day and to discuss the "circle of life".

Milestone:

Children need a mother and a father if at all possible. It was God's plan from the beginning. The memories we make for our children will become their milestones for tomorrow. We must do everything within our power to keep our families intact. And with God's help, it can be done.

I have so many memories of Rick it could be another book. But I'll let Rick write those in his book. We have shared an incredible life together and there's so much more to look forward to. Gray hair, no hair, menopause, arthritis. No, I'm just kidding.

Should God tarry, we'll watch our girls continue to grow and be used of God and then, maybe we'll even get a little more time for ourselves again.

One memory especially sticks out in my mind. Rick has always been so successful at everything he does. I know it is with God's help and anointing in his life that this is so. But, when we were pastoring in Grand Rapids, I saw Rick growing, becoming more sensitive to people's needs and creative in reaching the lost. It was an incredible time. Oh, we went on trips and took vacations. We walked on the white sandy beaches of Puerto Vallarta at sunset. We parasailed together over the bluegreen oceans of Mexico. We took an adventure on an abandoned road on the edge of the cliffs of Maui and saw the complete fossil of a dolphin or whale washed ashore. We've had candlelight dinners in fine restaurants above the tallest towers in metropolitan cities. We've sipped cappuccino under an open umbrella at a little sidewalk cafe on the streets of Paris. We've been to the Opera and to the Grand Ole' Opry. We've snow skied in Canada and jet skied at Fa-Ho-Lo Family Camp. We've cried together and laughed till we cried. It has been incredible!

But, in Grand Rapids, in the middle of building a house, building an annex to the church, "growing" a congregation and harvesting souls. Meeting with architects and counseling with alcoholics, my hero, my husband, the father of my children, took time out from all of this to have a picnic with us right in his office. I took a blanket and some Kentucky Fried chicken and some sweet iced tea, and the girls and said, "We need you." He shut his office door, told his secretary to hold all calls and we had a picnic, we ate, we laughed, we made a memory, and it was wonderful.

Milestone:

When life's routine gets overwhelming, TAKE TIME OUT, TOGETHER! The strangers will come and go and the problems to solve will wait, but the time spent showing your fam-

ily that you care will be an investment which will generate an eternity of rewards.

Next to the Lord, Rick has been my hero. Someone who rescues me when I'm in need and loves me even when I'm unlovely. I guess you could say I'm still infatuated with my "Italian Stallion"! The answer to my prayer and one of the special loves of my life.

CHAPTER 21

Funny Memory / Vacation Milestone

Everybody probably has vacation memories. Some good, some not so good. For Rick and his brothers and sister, their vacation memories consist of camping, wet tents and lots of bologna sandwiches. To this day, none of them will eat bologna.

For The Rick and Jennifer family, we've had some incredible journeys.

Taking our first vacation as a married couple to Niagara Falls, Canada. We saved and saved for that. Paid cash for our hotel for the whole week in advance. It was going to be ROMANTIC!

On the first day, we went to the Maid of the Mist and I left my purse in the car, along with the rest of our money. I didn't want to lose it on the boat. When we got back to the parking lot, our beautiful new 1979 White, T-top, Thunderbird had been broken in to. Glass everywhere. Purse and all the money, gone. Vacation over. Romance delayed. We did get our money back from the hotel, taped some cardboard over the window and went home.

Milestone:
Don't use cash on vacation, use traveler's checks. Don't leave your purse in the car. And as Rick said, don't give the money to the wife. (He's compromised on this area, since.)

Standing at the bottom of the Eiffel Tower in Paris, France, with a million people on Bastille day, four year old Jacklyn on top of someone's shoulders so she wouldn't get crushed by the crowd; not knowing that at that very minute God was beginning to give Jacklyn a view of the world because He would call her to the mission field and ask her to reach her world.

Taking Jacklyn and Jessica to Marco Island, Florida; Daddy Rick doing all the cooking, sitting out on the balcony and watching a school of dolphins swim by at sunset and feeling very happy and safe with our little family of four. It was one of the best vacations.

Watching all three of my girls, Jacklyn, Jessica, and Ericka; ages 9, 6, and 3; all dressed up in clown costumes running around a sandy park in the middle of Granada, Spain, spreading joy and laughter and the love of Jesus to little children in that park. Watching Jacklyn, walk around the perimeter of the park, praying for the teenagers that were with us, as they witnessed one on one to Spanish teenagers about the hope of Christ. Her view of the world expanding. Jessica, doing gymnastics on the swing sets with other little Spanish children, telling them Jesus loves you, want to pray? Ericka, mesmerized by the Mime skits; her love for the dramatic, growing. She could be a Christian actress. Actually, she already is.

And finally, the vacation from Hell. It was to be Ericka's big eight year old birthday celebration. She planned it with us. We were going to Disney World and she was going to see Mickey Mouse. We bought the tickets and set the date. Her birthday is March 29.

It was still very cold in Michigan, so all the summer clothes were still in storage. But, there would be time to sort through and get some shorts out for this hot vacation. The tickets came several weeks early, so we knew we were going.

It was Easter break. The girls would be out of school on Friday, we would leave at noon and have ten glorious days in Orlando.

As usual, I had been very busy and decided I would just pack on Thursday night. The girls were old enough, so they could help me get the clothes out of storage. We'd have time.

Thursday morning, Ericka woke up with a severe earache. I called the doctor and took her in about 10:00 a.m. She had a double ear infection. "Good thing you're not leaving until tomorrow," the doctor told me, "that way, she can have 24 hours on antibiotics before you fly. If you were flying today, her eardrums would probably rupture."

On the way home, we were going to stop by the pharmacy and get the prescription filled. As I pulled into the parking lot, my car phone rang. It was about 11:25 a.m. It was Rick. "Jen, we're not going to Florida." "What do you mean?", I replied, "Of course, we're going." "No, in 35 minutes, we're going to miss our flight." Rick said. "Our flight doesn't leave until tomorrow, dear. This is Thursday." , I said, feeling just a little panicky. "Jennifer, I looked at the tickets wrong. They were for today. Our flight leaves in 35 minutes.", the sadness and frustration in his voice, made me know that this was beginning of the nightmare.

At this point, Ericka was starting to pick up on the conversation and she started to cry, actually to wail, "We're not going to Disney World, my birthday is ruined." I tried to quiet Ericka and still hear Rick through the static of the car phone. My mind was racing and my blood pressure was rising. I needed this vacation, too.

Rick said all the other flights were overbooked because of Easter and Spring Break. Since it was our mistake, to change our tickets would have cost an additional $1500. We could go, but we wouldn't have any money to do anything. If we did go, it would have to be three days from now, cutting our vacation time considerably. That was not acceptable. The *only* possibility was for me to go to the airport and PLEAD our case and *maybe*, we could get out on stand-by the next day.

As I hung up the phone and wheeled the car out of the parking lot, I was trying to consider my options. Remember, I had not packed anything. And there are four girls in this family. "Okay," I thought, "I'm going to make this happen, with a serious amount of help from a gracious and merciful God who cares about our EVERY need."

I headed home.

I got right on the phone to the girls' schools. I told them we were about to miss our vacation and I had to pick the girls up early. "Have them waiting at the door." I swung by the Middle School and picked up Jacklyn, then by the elementary school and picked up Jessica. The girls were wondering what in the world was going on. "What's the big rush? We're not leaving until tomorrow,", Jessica said.   I told them we had thirty minutes to go home, get the summer clothes out of the basement, pack, put the St. Bernard dog in the garage, drive to Dad's office, drive to the airport and try to catch our plane. The airport is forty five minutes from our house.

As you read this, you're probably thinking, "I would have just given up. " I'll admit trying to cram two hours worth of activity into thirty minutes did seem like a totally futile endeavor, but I wanted this vacation and Ericka was still crying about her birthday being "ruined".

As we drove in the driveway, I told the girls to run in, grab a swimsuit, pj's, a couple shorts, and some underwear and stuff it in a suitcase. I told Jessica to grab Rick's golf clubs. I knew that if we did get to go, it wouldn't be a vacation for Rick without those clubs. You got to get the necessities.

I called Rick back at work and told him we were on our way. "You're crazy", he told me, "there's no way you're going to make it and even if we get another ticket, it won't be until tomorrow".

"I don't care, we've got to try", I told him. "If we do get on a standby, and you're not with us, what good would that do? We're doing this together."

We raced into the office parking lot, beeped the horn, and Rick ran out and jumped in. "This is crazy!" I think we all said it at the same time. "Did you bring my clubs?" "Yes, babe."

When we got to the airport, we took all our suitcases and everything right up to the ticket counter. I asked the clerk if the plane had left yet. We were forty minutes late. She looked at me like I was "crazy" and said, "Ma'am, the plane left forty minutes ago." What can I say? I was hoping that for once, the airlines would be off schedule and it would work to MY advantage.

I showed her Ericka's prescriptions and told her that we had to rush to the doctor with ear infection. This could be classified as a "medical emergency", couldn't it? Could they get us on the next flight?

She informed us that all flights to Florida were about fifty passengers overbooked. (Why do the airlines do this?) Anyway, she could put us on standby, send our luggage on and we could see what would happen. If we didn't make the flight, our luggage would have a great time in Florida without us. It was risky at best, and most likely impossible. Who knows how many standbys are already on the list ahead of you. A lot of students fly standby for Spring break because it's cheaper. I insisted that she let us try.

We had fifteen minutes to try to catch our breath and PRAY. We got to the gate and waited. And waited, and waited, and waited. With every passenger that showed up and boarded the plane, Ericka would start to cry again, "It's ruined! I won't even have a birthday."

Finally, the guy at the gate counter said there were seven seats left. He started calling standby names. "Johnson, Calvin" We were so tense, I thought we'd all explode. He knew we were waiting. He looked at Ericka and said, "Are you with the Pasquale family?" She started screaming and jumping up and down. We were on the plane in less than ten seconds.

As I sighed with relief, Rick looked over at me and said, "You know, we have to go through this again in St. Louis. When you fly standby, you have to do it on each leg of the journey." I could not believe it.

Well, when we got to St. Louis, it was the same scenario. Tension, waiting, passengers boarding as we waited some more. Names were called, not ours and we waited.

Finally, with only five seats left, the gate clerk started calling the Standby list. There were seven names in front of us. "This IS crazy!" I thought, "now we're just going to be stuck in St. Louis and our luggage is already in Florida". Suddenly, he was calling, "Pasquale, party of five". It felt like Christmas! We were all laughing and jumping and hugging. We were going to Florida. God is so good!

When we finally arrived in Florida, it had been several long hours since the hectic day had started. Don't forget Ericka's double ear infection. Luckily, I had some Tylenol with me and I had given that to her on the plane. She was so happy to be on the plane, that she didn't even complain about her ears popping. I had been in such a hurry that I had left the house with no jewelry, very little makeup and no idea of what had actually gotten thrown in the suitcases.

I had also forgotten to do anything with the dog. You can

not leave a St. Bernard in the garage by itself for ten days. I called a friend to go get the dog, take it in her car and take it to the kennel. She did and she's still my friend.

We also had parked our car in short term parking, thinking we would be getting back in it because we wouldn't get on a flight today. So, we called another friend, tried to describe where the car was parked, asked him to go to Rick's office and get the extra set of keys that had luckily been left on Rick's desk, go get the car and take it home with him. Then, he'd pick us up next week. This would save us a lot of money in parking. He did and he's still our friend.

When we arrived at the hotel, they didn't have our room ready. We ended up taking a single room for the first night and the girls slept on the floor. It's amazing how when you finally get something you had to work really hard for, the little inconveniences don't seem to matter. We were in Florida and we were going to have fun! The expression, "Are we having fun yet?" took on new meaning.

The rest of the trip went great. We had a wonderful family time, Rick got to go golfing, and Ericka had her birthday celebration.

Then, it was time to go home. This trip to the airport would be much more relaxed, we'd be packed properly, relaxed from our vacation and ready to go. We arrived at the Orlando airport in plenty of time and headed home. And we didn't have to wait for our name to be called. (By the way, we didn't have to pay any extra for the ticket changes.)

As the plane was making it's touch down in St. Louis, I could feel myself getting nauseous. When the ramp was hooked up and the plane doors were opened, I literally pushed past passengers and ran off the plane to the nearest restroom and threw up. I was sick. About thirty minutes later, green and woozy, I walked out to find the family. Rick just shook his head and we headed for the next gate to make the connection to Detroit and Home, Sweet Home.

We were told at the gate that the plane was delayed and we'd have to wait about one hour. I was so sick, I just grabbed my jacket, made a pillow and curled up on the floor and tried to rest. After an hour, Rick was told, another hour. After six hours, we were told the flight was canceled. We were not going home.

We could not believe this. Jacklyn said, "This is the vacation that couldn't start and won't stop." We got a taxi, found a hotel and crashed, literally, for the night. Again, our luggage was already where it was supposed to be.

When we got up in the morning, we caught the first plane out and headed home. We called our friend about the car. He had gotten our return flight schedule from Rick's secretary and had waited until about 2:00 in the morning for us to arrive. Which, we never did, because that flight had been canceled. He left the car, told us about where to find it and got another ride home.

When we got to Detroit, we found our luggage, eventually found the car, went by and picked up the St. Bernard, and went home to bed.

Was this vacation meant to be? Was it worth the hassle? Yes, Yes! My kids will never forget it. We can laugh about it now and it makes a great story to tell. A vacation full of memories.

Milestone:
Even when it seems impossible, don't give up! Stress revs up the adrenaline and the adrenaline helps you get it done. Stress is not always bad. Vacations are not always stress free.

Milestone:
Always LOOK AT YOUR TICKETS when they arrive. Double check all travel arrangements. Put a few items of necessity

in your carry - on bag. Look at problems as possibilities. Where there's a will there's a way.

Milestone:

Vacations are a time for family, for making memories that become stepping stones in the foundation of our lives. Life can not be all work and no play. Even Jesus rested. God rested after He created the world. Adam slept in the garden. Take time to refresh yourself and your family. It can be the adhesive that glues us back together. It doesn't have to be long and it doesn't have to be expensive. It just requires time and in our society scheduling. It is just as important as your best client or your Final exam. It deserves a date on the calendar. It's worth it. Your family is worth it.

CHAPTER 22

Memory Makers & Milestone Builders

Grandma Pasquale, Grandma Blythe, Papa Schaffer, Aunt Joyce, Aunt Susie, Bro. Way, Bro. Goree, Mike Cave, Anita Bellers, Barry Edgemon, Tina Wilson, Penny and Kelvin, Kelly Utt, Kim Utt, Ken and Merilee, Steve and Mary Miramonti, Tim Foote, Chris Cramer, Ken Whittum, Ken Hubbard, Randy and Lori DonGiovanni, Phil DiMusto, Paul Kirschbaum, Leachs, Muhlings, dozens of youth pastors, dozens of fellow ministers, all of our family.

This chapter is about all of the people that contribute to our lives. The funny memories they leave behind, for us to enjoy, and the milestone lessons they give us that help to build our lives.

As you reflect with me on those who have impacted my life, I hope you will reflect upon those who have helped make you a better person today.

I recently heard Kathie Lee Gifford express this thought, "I am who I am today because of those who have loved me, but I will be what I am to become because of those that I will love."

Looking back, makes us thankful for all those who have invested in our lives and stepping forward happens, when we decide to make investments of our own into those we have opportunity to touch.

You might almost call this chapter, "Name dropping". There is no way I could ever drop every name that has affected my life. It's not important if your name is written in Jen's book, but it is of eternal importance, to make sure your name is written in the "Lamb's Book of Life".

The name, the memory, the milestone:

Grandma Pasquale, teaching me to make authentic Italian pasta, wedding soup, and praying around the family table: prayer is the ultimate legacy to pass on to your family. Rick's grandma was born in Italy and she has kept the fun Italian traditions alive in our family. Her faithfulness to God has been an example to all who know her.

Aunt Joyce and Uncle Jimmy, spanking me for slamming the door on my brother, being there for my children and loving them as their own grandchildren, keeping Mother close to me by staying close to me themselves, even though hundreds of miles separate us: anger solves nothing, and families stay close by constantly tightening the knots that keep us together.

I lived with Aunt Joyce, Uncle Jimmy and my two cousins, Cande and Penny after Mother died. It was a difficult time that year in school, there. I really don't remember much about that. But, I do know that those months with them built a relationship that has stayed strong through the years.

Aunt Joyce has been like a mother to me and like another grandmother to my children. We love to go to her house and make crafts, have BIG family parties with skits and lots of laughing, and just relax with family. We don't get to go as often as we used to, but distance is the only thing that separates us. When I've gone through hard times, Aunt Joyce has always been faithful to send me little "pick you up" notes, funny cards, and make phone calls to see how I'm doing.

Aunt Joyce has been so faithful to the Lord and her family. She has helped so many, especially me, to keep on the right path.

I remember one time when I was a child. Aunt Joyce had taken all of us kids to the shopping mall. We were standing in the middle of the mall trying to decide what to do next. It was the holiday season and there were lots of people in the mall. All of a sudden, Aunt Joyce just broke out in song. It wasn't just softly singing under her breath. She was singing "You are My Sunshine" at the top of her lungs, a melody that would have made Minnie Pearl proud. However, we were not proud. We were so embarrassed, at first. Then, we were all singing and laughing and EVERYONE in the mall was looking at our entourage to see what the "commotion" was all about. It was just one of many occurrences where Aunt Joyce made the routine event an extraordinary memory!

Everybody has fun with Aunt Joyce.

Milestone:
It doesn't take much to make the ordinary routine, extraordinarily wonderful! Love life with all you have and make use of every ingredient.

Grandma Schaffer Blythe means the world to me. There are too many memories and milestones I've learned in her presence to record them all.

I can remember her singing and praising God as she went about her day, from the time I was probably only three or four years old, until now, at her age of 82. I have never heard her say a bad word about anybody. She has become everybody's Grandma.

At age 82, she resigned from her full-time State position with the Tennessee Assemblies of God, after 35 years. She didn't stop or retire, though. She took on a full time Associate Pastor position at Cornerstone Assembly of God church in Nashville, Tennessee. The church runs over one thousand in attendance and Grandma is still keeping office hours and ministering weekly. (I told you earlier she could still run circles around me.) She is just absolutely the most incredible, Godly woman I have or will ever know.

She has prayed with me, laughed with me, cried with me, and kept me supplied with wonderful words of insight throughout my life.

She used to tell me the story of Epandimondes when I was little, she sings original songs to all of her great grandchildren, she loves to play rook and dominoes and she and I always make great partners.

The heritage that she has instilled in each of us has been an investment on her part and the returns were ours. My Jacklyn gets her preaching and speaking skills from her great grandmother, making Jacklyn a fourth generation Pentecostal preacher. My Jessica loves to sit at Grandma's feet and listen to her sing songs and tell stories. My Ericka Jane is named after Grandma - Alice Jane. (Michael's daughter is also named Jane).

One of the memories I share sometimes is about when I called Grandma, one of the millions of calls I've made to her, to ask for guidance. She has always been a wonderful listener and a great encourager. But, this particular time, I guess she was busy with District events. I shared with her some frustrations I was having with my stubborn Italian husband. She quickly replied, "Well, honey, you just have to take it to Jesus. Gotta go. Love you." And she hung up.

I couldn't believe it. I needed Grandma's wisdom and all she could say was, "Take it to Jesus." Do you know those have been the wisest four words anyone has ever said to me. Well, I did take it to Jesus and He gave me some really creative ways of talking to Rick. I did them, and all the frustrations were resolved in peace and harmony and I didn't even cry.

That's what I mean about Grandma. She's just awesome!

Milestone:
If I could only remember to "Take it to Jesus" every time I get frustrated in life. It seems we always think we need someone else to hear our woes and sympathize with us. Sometimes, it's nice to hear a verbal voice on the other end, but it's always more productive and beneficial to me personally, when I listen for that "still small Voice" that speaks to my heart and helps bring peace to my mind. The Bible does say, that He will give us "peace that passes understanding". You won't get that promise from any friend or psychologist. Grandma has given me the tools to make my milestones be the foundation that God intended for them to be.

Papa Schaffer, falling off the ladder while painting the garage and spilling paint all over the driveway, golfing with Rick until the Lord took him home, pastoring churches where people loved him so much that they never lost contact with him and the pastors who succeeded him always wanted him back for special events: life is fun, be able to laugh, keep going, serve others with integrity and your life will be full of friendship.

Brenda Powell, an adult youth sponsor who took the time to invest in a teenager's "infatuation" and was used by God to put Rick and I together: match-making has it's value and "infatuations" should be taken seriously.

Mike and Sharon Cave, a youth pastor and his wife who invested hundreds of hours, miles, phone bills, laughs, hugs, and prayers into the lives of hurting and confused teens: no life should be ignored, not every investment is obvious, but the dividends can multiply for generations.

Anita Bellers, a dear friend and caretaker of my children. Anita was someone we invested time in while we were youth pastors in Ypsilanti. She became one of our leaders and began watching Jacklyn at age one.

Through every stage of our ministry, no matter the miles, Anita has been a true friend who was always there for us and our girls. She has taught all of us the meaning of giving of one's self. My children adore her.

Anita, herself, could write a book. She has been through many sad and disappointing events in her life, but she has never lost her love for children. That love is God-given and she continues to serve Him by faith.

I have been so blessed to have someone trustworthy to hand my children over to when we go out of town. She goes beyond the second mile, and way beyond that. There have been immeasurable returns on our investment of friendship with her.

Every pastor in our lives, every youth pastor friend we've worked with, young people we've had the privilege of knowing and watching grow and maybe even impacting their lives, cousins, neighbors, friends, and family; wonderful memories of building snowmen, being buried in the sand, weddings, car pooling, prayer meetings, instructional times; milestones of growing and watching grow - the life cycle is NOT boring but it is ever changing.

Change may not always be easy but eventually, it can be a passage way into the next adventure, the next memory, the next milestone on the path that leads to eternity. Where is your path leading you? And who is on your path and who is leading?

CHAPTER 23

Memories in the Making

My life continues to be a book in progress. Every week I "write" a new chapter. I guess you could say it's been kind of like the "ugly duckling/swan" syndrome.

As a child and young teenager, I always felt out of the loop, not a part, very insecure, but as I've become an adult, I've grown to appreciate the good God has created in me, learned how to use it to the best of my ability and learned not to give up when doubt tries to take control.

I'm still growing. Just like my eighty two year old grandmother who's still experiencing new things in life, I don't want to ever stop the adventure. It might be easier sometimes to just stick with the memories we have, and decide to live through reflection, but reflections fade. We can always make new memories, blaze new trails, conquer new challenges and sometimes finally conquer the old challenges. Life is growth and growth is change, don't be afraid of it, embrace it.

I've watched my daughters grow from precious, tiny, babies to beautiful "developing" young women. I'm coming to a point in time where I no longer have those reference memories.

Jacklyn will turn fifteen, and I was her age when I lost

my mother. Sometimes I think, "I don't know what to do next." I watched my mom for fifteen years, "now what?" But I do know that God pilots my ship, not the co-pilot as some bumper stickers say, but THE Pilot. And HIS WORD is my instruction manual.

I wonder as my mother looks down from above, "Is she proud of who I am?" I am continually guided by her words, as well. Not in a mysterious, spiritual way, but practically.

She left her Bible behind and my grandmother or maybe Regena, found it, and gave it to me. She had written so many words and thoughts in the flyleaves of her Bible. I have found so many answers in that Red, leather, Bible with the ruffled pages and the fading print. But, God's word never fades, His power never fails, His peace never falters, and His presence never falls short of keeping us in the palm of His care.

At the current time, Rick has been serving as the District Youth Director for the Assemblies of God, Michigan District. He oversees all of the youth related activities for the 260 churches in the state, the 9,000 teenagers in those churches, the 77 full time youth pastors and the countless part time and volunteer youth workers across Michigan.

We, as a family, are very involved in this ministry. Our girls with their various talents are always eager to be a part of what God is doing in our state.

We have made some wonderful friendships in these last five years. Our/Rick's boss, our District Superintendent and his terrific family, have been so wonderful to us. They helped through my surgery time, have given us freedom and opportunity to use our talents and creative energies for the Lord, and have made the "Team" we work with a family. It is a joy and privilege to serve God and others.

I was given the opportunity to decorate the 40,000 square feet of the District owned Office building, with Rick's supervision of course. It was a thrill and a challenge. Interior decorating becomes an increasing joy and interest of mine. I have had opportunities to speak on this subject at the schools and to help others as well. It is an ever developing talent the Lord is giving me. I do a lot of reading on the subject and have been "self-taught" and family inspired. My Aunt Joyce inspires creativity in everyone, especially me, and Rick's Aunt Monica does the same.

I stay active in my daughters' schools. This is very important because they are in the Public School system. It is important no matter what manner of education your child receives. We are our children's main source of information and guidance. Everything else is secondary. Psychologists will tell you that the environment in which the child lives affects them as much as their heredity. "God, help me to make their environment a place of learning and growing." Making sure to incorporate the Four L's: Love, Laughter, Listening, and Loyalty in every day.

As you stop and reflect in your own life, take a moment to remember the love someone shared with you. Realize the milestones that your memories have made and be thankful for the growing process. It is crucial to emotional contentment, that we do not harbor bitterness for the past. Bitterness robs us of joy and distorts our perspectives. Look back on the past with respect; respect for yourself, respect for who you have become because of the memories.

My memories are a part of who I am and will be a part of who I become as well as those I influence. Not all the memories are happy, but the Milestones are invaluable tools which help me grow.

Stop for a minute today. Create a memory and lay a foundational milestone in the lives of those around you. Look back, see where you've been, see where you've come and envision where you are going, step forward with joy and anticipation for the treasures and pleasures that wait for you just over the crest of the next mountain you climb.

Found on the flyleaf of my own worn and tattered red leather Bible with the faded edges and the tear stained pages, is what I want others to remember about me:

God has created me to do Him some definite service....
I am a link in a chain, a bond of connection between persons.
He has not created me for naught. I shall do good.....
If I am in sickness, my sickness may serve Him;
If I am in sorrow, my sorrow may serve Him,
He does nothing in vain....
He may take away my friends,
He may throw me among strangers.
He may make me feel desolate, make my spirit sick,
Hide my future from me, Still...
He knows what he is about. Amen.

by Cardinal Newman

EPILOGUE

Milestones Compiled

Milestone:
A life's calling was being formed in the mind of a child and stimulated by those who had opportunity to influence her life.

Milestone:
STABILITY

Milestone:
She was teaching me, through her example, that you can always improve, and still be a good steward of the talents and gifts God gives.

Milestone:
The stability of the past, was now keeping me stable in a supernatural way. I was losing one of the most precious gifts ever given to me and gaining another one at the same time, TRUST in the Giver of Gifts.

Milestone:
Sometimes, I think we feel useless in other's tragedies, therefore we do not allow ourselves to be used. But, just being there speaks even louder than words sometimes. Depend-

ability - horizontally and vertically; I must recognize, that between God and me, we can depend on each other, and I must also recognize, that between me and others, we can depend on each other.

Milestone:
To cry, showing a continued sensitivity. Not putting up a tough exterior. Remember, what you pretend, you later practice. A conscious decision to continue to trust God, not blame Him; to allow others to be in my life - this would be a character trait blossoming for the future.

Milestone:
The realization that she was gone, and making the choice to begin to step forward, one stone at a time.

Milestone:
When life's routine gets overwhelming, TAKE TIME OUT, TOGETHER! The strangers will come and go and the problems to solve will wait, but the time spent showing your family that you care will be an investment which will generate an eternity of rewards.

Milestone:
When God grabs hold of your life, He NEVER lets go. Even if you try to loosen your grip, He's still holding on.

Milestone:
The picture doesn't have to be perfect to be enjoyed. It's life's imperfections that make us appreciate the beauty. If we didn't have winter, with all it's gray, cold, and dreary days, and all the bare branches, we would never appreciate the fresh spring breeze, the newly blossoming plants, the new growth and the old growth being revived. That's what happens with change.

New growth in some areas. Other areas just get revived with time. Time does heal.

Milestone:
Anyone can contribute to a family, if given the opportunity. I'm thankful that I had mentors in my life encouraging me to give Regena a chance. To appreciate the value of BLENDING. Consequently, Regena encouraged my emotional growth, and helped me to continue improving my life skills.

Milestone:
You're never too old to get an education. Education is very important, even if you have to sacrifice to get it. AND, education is a life long pursuit.

Milestone:
A love for nature and all of God's creation. We now have a St. Bernard in our household. I wonder if Mother would have approved? (Sometimes, it's hard when memories can't answer questions for today. It's like not having enough information in the data bank to gather a conclusion. It's like being thrown in and THEN learning to swim, you just have to do the best you can.)

Milestone:
I could always talk to my father. In the future, there would be so many times when the Lord would use my earthly father to give me HIS divine guidance. When I accept the wisdom of the one whom God has placed over me, I am accepting God's wisdom - the umbrella of authority is protecting me from the elements.

Milestone:
Two things stick out in my data bank here. One, my earthly family is very precious. The blessing of being able to be depended on is a precious gift to pass down for generations. The Italians are very big on this. (another chapter) Two, just like the kitchen faucet causes me to remember Daddy. God's word causes us to remember His faithfulness in our lives. He wants us to use it just as much as the kitchen faucet. And every time we touch it, it is serving a different purpose in our lives. And every time we touch it, the Word, it should serve as a reminder that our Heavenly Father is there, He cares, and He will always come through.

Milestone:
Obeying God's direction may not be easy, but you often have help in the process. (I had Brenda and Rick) God's word for your life does not originate with others, but can be confirmed through them. When choosing a mate for life, spiritual cohesiveness must be a major priority in the relationship. The first step may be painful, but the ones that follow hold untold facets of excitement.

Milestone:
This was one of those times, when I realized how important my talk with Daddy had been. Those times, when it had been hard to say No, but I did, had paid off. I was about to get the man of my dreams, because I had stayed true to myself and to God. Anything worth having is worth waiting for. Something new always makes a better gift than something used.

Milestone:
Never try to figure out how God is going to accomplish His will in your life. Don't put God in a box, or in a State. He is Omnipresent, and He can move the hearts of people in differ-

ent places at different times for different events and ultimately blend it all together and create a masterpiece. Sometimes you have to go, before you know. Even Abraham had to follow God, without knowing where God was leading. But, it will always be confirmed through the Word of God.

Milestone:
Many things we don't understand in the present, are revealed as a part of God's plan later on. Again, the authority issue greatly affects our lives. Not only, if we obey the authority, but what is our attitude in the act of obedience? We must not stop living or put our lives on hold just because we can't see around the bend. In the car, we keep driving, by faith, trusting, that the road safely continues, always careful to follow the instruction signs along the way - Keep right. Caution! Stop. Proceed Slowly. Construction Completed, Continue on!

Milestone:
If you don't settle for second best, allow God to be the keeper of the time clock, and TRUST HIM, He always gives you the very best. Also, when you need something from the Lord, meet Him face to Face. Or faith to Face. He said in Psalms 37, "Delight thyself also in the Lord; and he shall give thee the desires of thine heart. Commit thy way unto the Lord; trust also in him; and he shall bring it to pass."

Milestone:
Sometimes, it's the little things that help us in practical ways. The checkbook, the house cleaning, the game. I was learning to appreciate the things that would make my house run more smoothly. Some things you learn now, but don't use until later.

Milestone:
Even if the purpose of God's plan is not revealed along the way, there is good in every situation. But there is one condition: you get what you put in to it. Life is a process of investments and returns, deposits and withdrawals. When the account gets low, you have to take the time to build up the equity again. If you don't, you will move so swiftly along the road, that you miss the landmarks of beauty along the way. You might get there quicker than I do, but at whose expense? And with how much enjoyment? Remember, five steps forward and two steps back is still only three steps. However, as long as you are moving ahead, you're going in the right direction. Never give up!

Milestone:
Even though restrictions can be restricting, we learned that it is very important to look your best. This body is the temple of the Holy Spirit, and we should not get lazy in taking care of it. Outward appearances draw people to you, if the appearance is good. Then, the inward appearance of your life draws them to Christ.

Milestone:
Never think, "I'm not good enough". Creator God makes no mistakes. It may sound corny, but He's more interested in our availability than our ability. "Not by might, nor by power, but by HIS Spirit."

Milestone:
If you're willing to do whatever, for the Lord, He will take the investment and triple the returns. Mentors are important, too. A mentor is someone who invests time, leadership, friendship, and personal commitment into another's life, not for the temporal rewards, but for the sake of eternity.

Milestone:
God is no respector of persons. Acts 10:34, Peter made this statement after he had betrayed Christ. He was realizing Christ's forgiveness in his own life. It doesn't matter who you are, who your parents are, what you did or what you do, the Blood covers it all.

Milestone:
He always has a plan, no matter how far away we get from it. II Corinthians 9:8, "And God is able to make all grace abound toward you; that ye, always having all sufficiency in all things, may abound to every good work."

Milestone:
Teaching life skills does not have to come out of a text book. In fact, some of the best training you can receive, can be done by watching someone else. Don't be afraid to ask questions. (Mom always has an ear to hear. Even if she doesn't have the answer, she's a terrific listener.) Parents need to listen as much as talk. You teach self-esteem when you validate another's opinions just by listening.

Milestone:
Proverbs 16:9, "A man's heart deviseth his way: but the Lord directeth his steps."

Milestone Remembered:
Faith to Face. This was the biggest crisis the Pasquales had faced, and now we had to face God with our faith in His ability to take control of the situation.

Milestone:
God is sovereign! He is in control! He won't give us more than we are able to bear! He will push us to the limit, or at least, allow us to be pushed. He is as close as the mention of His name. I trust God, not because of what He does, but because of who He is. Remember, in order to look forward, we have to look back, at the cross. We have to look at Christ's sufferings. Christ cried out to His Father, "Why hast thou forsaken me?" He knows our pain, he feels our sorrow, he suffered our afflictions. I Corinthians 15:57, "But thanks be to God, which giveth us the victory through our Lord Jesus Christ." I Corinthians 13:7, "Love beareth all things, believeth all things, hopeth all things, endureth all things." I John 4:8, "God is love." Seek God in the midst of EVERY situation, good and bad. Jeremiah 29:11-13, "For I know the thoughts that I think toward you, saith the Lord, thoughts of peace, and not of evil, to give you an expected end. Then shall ye call upon me, and ye shall go and pray unto me, and I will hearken unto you. And ye shall seek me, and find me, when ye shall search for me with all your heart." No matter what, I must seek God. I can not make it through life's difficulties without Him and I do not want to experience life's goodness apart from Him.

Milestone:
Never give up in the face of adversity. Sometimes, even death seems easier. "But to live is Christ and to die is gain" Until God calls each of us home, to live for Him is to live a life, abundant and full.

Milestone:
Never give up! "The effectual, fervent prayers of a righteous man, availeth much." Even when they are prayed for the unrighteous. Keep loving your children, no matter what they

do. *Even if they disappoint you, you are their parent. Just like our relationship with Father God. Even when we disappoint Him, He's still the one who gave us life. We are linked for eternity.*

Milestone:
The stamina required to be a parent for life, make that a good parent for life, has to be supernaturally given. If you're trying to make it without Divine Intervention, you're not using all the blocks available. The Word of God gives instructions to the parents, It gives comfort to the parent who feels the despair of the situation, It gives hope to the hopeless, It gives strength to the weary, It is the blueprint for life. The ultimate book on "Blended Families". Why wouldn't you use it? At least, read it. Through everything, I have never seen Mom lose her faith. I have never heard her blame God. I'm sure she's had her private talks with Him, but she continues to trust Him.

Milestone:
Parents must accept their children even when they don't do what we would have expected for them. Forgiveness is an action, not a conversation. Someone once said you should raise a child with the four L's: Love, listening, laughter, and loyalty. Mom had practiced all of these with Jeff and the others, but with Jeff, especially loyalty.

Milestone:
Mother/daughter relationships take a lot of work. Women can be very emotional and unpredictable at times. I've been a daughter, now I'm a mother to daughters, and I've watched numerous other mother/daughter relationships. There has to be give and take on both sides of the relationship. We must

try to put ourselves in each other's shoes, from time to time. It will help the understanding process, immensely. Daughters need independence from their mothers. Mothers want to hold their daughters, (even their sons), forever. Moms need to give their daughters space once in a while and daughters need to give more hugs. The "Momma bird" prepares a nest for her babies, before they come. She stays in the nest while they are developing. She feeds them, sings to them, teaches them to fly, to soar. Then, she lets them go. The "baby bird" never returns to the "mom's" nest. In fact, the baby bird goes and begins another cycle of life. We could take a lesson from these little creatures of "Father" God. Luke chapter 12 reminds us, that not one sparrow is overlooked by God. He knows when they drop from the nest. As "Momma birds", we must begin to trust "Father" God to watch over our little "sparrows" for us, after they "drop from our nests". No need to worry, God is in control!

Milestone:

As I have observed Joan Pasquale, over the last eighteen years, I have learned so much. I have enjoyed her company, appreciated her support, and cherished the memories in the making. She has shown me that right priorities, help keep your life in perspective. If your priorities are straight, you just take circumstances, one stone at a time. Sometimes, it might feel like you're being "stoned", other times, you might wish you were "stoned", and other times, it will seem as though all the stones are creating a great masterpiece of artwork. It's called the tapestry of life. There are many textures, many fabrics and colors, many seemingly insignificant threads, and other beautifully ornate threads interwoven to make the magnificent cording that frames the piece. There are many lives interwoven in ours that make us God's masterpiece. If one thread begins to unravel, you could lose the whole fabric. That's why every thread is important, though, not always seen or recognized by those that gaze upon the masterpiece. These are few of those unseen threads in Joan's life that have been woven together to create a masterpiece of love and gentleness. I love you, Mom!

Milestone:
It is important to build relationships with the people you work with. "No man is an island". It's a lot more fun to serve those who appreciate us in a variety of ways. It is also a lot easier to lead those whom you have invested personal time with. No, this is not risky! In our society today, we must have those in our lives to whom we can be accountable. It will keep us pure, in thought, motive, action, and deed.

Milestone:
In the ministry, it is imperative that your spouse becomes your best friend. Friendships are built upon giving. I had to learn to give support, not instruction. (Like I really knew more than Rick. He was the preacher's kid, I was the engineer's kid. I do have good ideas though. I just had to learn how and when to express them.) Rick had to learn to accept me and to nurture my gifts and talents. There's a fine line between leading and dragging. Rick was learning to lead. I developed the ability to sing. Talents aren't always inherited. Sometimes they are learned, always with practice.

Milestone:
You are never too old to take instruction from your father. (Especially, when he's your boss.) Family loyalty is one of the most precious gifts you can give to your children. (Mom and Dad were always there, supporting our ministry efforts. That meant so much.) Family dinners make the best opportunity for family milestones. Everyone sitting down to eat, at the same time, at the same table, is an art that must not be forgotten. (This family has the BEST spaghetti in the world!)

Milestone:
If you're willing to let God open some unexpected doors, you will experience some unexpected joys. Flexibility is the key to a happy and UNfrustrated life. You can call it adventure or adversity. It's up to your attitude. This was an adventure. Also, God blesses those who give. This was a time of tremendous blessing.

Milestone:
There is learning to be done in every situation. If I'm not learning, I'm probably not growing. The blessings of God come in a variety of packages, through a variety of people. Never turn away the "little" packages, sometimes they contain the best surprises. Never minimize the giftings in other people. Strong leaders help others maximize their talents.

Milestone:
Talk to your wife, before you take away her "nest"! Let your husband lead and follow with joy! If a mistake gets made, he'll be responsible for it. Include the ENTIRE family in the decisions that affect them.

Milestone:
Giving birth, especially for the first time, is the most awesome involvement in a miracle you could ever have. Having a husband to share that experience, is the most wonderful expression of two becoming one. Having Jacklyn was another dream fulfilled for me. Now, I would have a real baby doll to go to church with me.

Milestone:
Rejoicing in the accomplishments of our children is thrilling. I can just barely imagine how Father God must rejoice when His children accomplish the goals He has for them. I want to

be that kind of child to Father God and Jacklyn was setting an example for me. Kids teach parents, too, sometimes.

Milestone:
Sometimes it is so hard to really give our kids to the Lord. I was thinking, "God, you can have her when she's grown, but she's just a kid, not now." But God is so faithful! When we let Him have them, He does more with their hearts and attitudes than we could do in a thousand conversations with them. He is the ultimate parental authority and we as His children, must trust Him with ALL our lives.

Milestone:
Our children are never too young to begin learning God's plan for their lives. They are not too young to understand eternity or too young to make choices affecting their eternity. We MUST give children the opportunity to be introduced to God and His great plans and then allow them to make an educated choice about whom they will serve. "Bring up a child in the way he should go, and when he is old, he will not depart from it." Our society needs values and children need parents with values to teach them. We can ALL "Bloom where we're planted", no matter the age.

Milestone:
Kids are human too. No matter what their academic status or social maturity, they must be allowed to have their childhood. There is a fine balance between pushing them towards excellence and giving them the space for imperfections. Raising children is God's way of allowing us as parents, to practice the fruits of mercy and tolerance. The four L's: Love, laughter, listening, and loyalty. A time for all seasons and sometimes, all seasons in one time. What a juggling act.

Milestone:
Sometimes, we feel like an insignificant speck. Could God really care about our little wishes and dreams? YES! We are his sparrows. He knows when we fall and when we fly and He is there at all times. He grants our desires on a level that enables us to see God right where we're at and He meets our needs in the most unexpected ways. I'm sure Peter never expected to walk on water. I'm sure Mary never expected to have a baby without a husband. I'm sure the people never expected to see Lazarus after he was put in that tomb. I'm sure the disciples never expected to talk with the resurrected Lord. But, God goes beyond our highest expectations. We can't designate our miracle specifications. If we could, it wouldn't be a miracle. We must be on the lookout for God to do the unexpected and receive our miracles. Jessica got hers and so did the stranger with the gymnastic ticket. God is no respector of persons.

Milestone:
Always hang up your clothes when you take them off.

Milestone:
Jesus said, "Let the little children come to me?" He said, "a child shall lead them". We must give our children the opportunity to experience God for themselves. You don't have to be an adult to understand God. You don't have to be a child to experience His "parenting". God has taught me so much through this third, born gift. And believe me, it is a never ending, educational experience.

Milestone:
The athlete knows discipline, his coach makes sure of that. But, when his team wins the championship, he understands the discipline. Someday, we're going to win the FINAL Cham-

pionship and I want to make sure my kids are on the winning team.

Milestone:
Discipline is a necessity of life. I wonder how many times the Lord would like us to recite the Ten Commandments. Forgive and it shall be forgiven you. Just like little children, we forget, we fail, sometimes we even forsake. But like the loving parent, He forgives, He restores us in to right relationship and He never stops loving us.

Milestone:
God knows our deepest and innermost thoughts. Nothing is a secret to Him. When we are desperate, He delivers hope.

Milestone:
God is sovereign. We can not demand He answer our prayers our way, but we must expect Him to answer according to His word. Does he cure cancer every time? No Why? I don't know. But I do know that we have not because we ask not. And I also know we must ask, according to His will, not ours.

Milestone:
Realizing that a crisis can bring out the best and the worst in us. It is very important to trust God during these times based on faith not feelings. Remember, face to Faith. Standing on the promises because He tells me to , not always because I feel confident. Faith, "the substance of things hoped for, the evidence of things NOT seen".

Milestone:
Many of us go through experiences in our lives that require a recovery period. What we do in the recovery process is up to us. We can try to turn and run, perhaps too fast, and end up

falling; or we can stand with arms outstretched reaching for God's hand that is extended to pull us through. Though we don't understand each circumstance, God is in control. We have to pace ourselves and respect the healing process. Time heals. With time scars fade, pains go away and strength is regained.

Milestone:
Don't use cash on vacation; use traveler's checks. Don't leave your purse in the car. And as Rick said, don't give the money to the wife. (He's compromised on this area, since.)

Milestone:
Even when it seems impossible, don't give up! Stress revs up the adrenaline and the adrenaline helps you get it done. Stress is not always bad. Vacations are not always stress free.

Milestone:
Always LOOK AT YOUR TICKETS when they arrive. Double check all travel arrangements. Put a few items of necessity in your carry - on bag. Look at problems as possibilities. Where there's a will there's a way.

Milestone:
Vacations are a time for family, for making memories that become stepping stones in the foundation of our lives. Life can not be all work and no play. Even Jesus rested. God rested after He created the world. Adam slept in the garden. Take time to refresh yourself and your family. It can be the adhesive that glues us back together. It doesn't have to be long and it doesn't have to be expensive. It just requires time and in our society scheduling. It is just as important as your best client or your Final exam. It deserves a date on the calendar. It's worth it. Your family is worth it.

Milestone:
So many times we fail to pray, believing that God really cares about the desires of our hearts. But, if we would only take HIM literally at HIS word, and OBEY, His endless treasures could be ours. "Delight thyself also in the Lord; and he shall give thee the desires of thine heart. Commit thy way unto the Lord; trust also in him; and he shall bring IT to pass." Psalms 37:4,5

Milestone:
Children need a mother and a father if at all possible. It was God's plan from the beginning. The memories we make for our children will become their milestones for tomorrow. We must do everything within our power to keep our families intact. And with God's help, it can be done.

Milestone:
When life's routine gets overwhelming, TAKE TIME OUT, TOGETHER! The strangers will come and go and the problems to solve will wait, but the time spent showing your family that you care will be an investment which will generate an eternity of rewards.